is the P...
Mensa Magazine

Philip Carter
is Puzzle Editor of *Enigmasig,*
the puzzle special interest group within Mensa

What Is Mensa?

Mensa is a unique society. It is, basically, a social club — but a social club different from others. The only qualification for membership is a high score on an intelligence test. One person in fifty should qualify for membership; these people will come from all walks of life and have a wide variety of interests and occupations.

Mensa is the Latin word for table: we are a round-table society where no one has special precedence. We fill a void for many intelligent people otherwise cut off from contact with other good minds — contact that is important to them, but elusive in modern society. Besides being an origin of many new friendships, we provide members with a receptive but critical audience on which to try out new ideas.

Mensa is protean: its most visible feature is its diversity. It crosses the often artificial barriers which separate people from each other. It recruits, not like other societies by persuading people to think as they do, or by searching for a particular narrow common interest, but by scientifically selecting people who are able to think for themselves. Yet, although there appears little common ground and little surface agreement between members, we find there is an underlying unity which gives an unexpected strength to the society.

Mensa has three aims: social contact between intelligent people; research in psychology and the social sciences; and the identification and fostering of human intelligence. Mensa is an international society; it has more than 85,000 members. We have members of almost every occupation — business people, clerks, doctors, editors, factory workers, farm labourers, housewives, lawyers, police officers, politicians, soldiers, scientists, students, teachers — and of almost every age.

Enquiries and applications to:

Mensa
FREEPOST
Wolverhampton WV2 1BR

Mensa International
15 The Ivories
6-8 Northampton Street
London N1 2HV

Acknowledgements

This book is dedicated to our wives, both named Barbara, for their encouragement and assistance in helping to prepare the questions in the verbal tests and for checking and typing the manuscript.

We wish to thank Harold Gale and Victor Serebriakoff, both of whom are prolific puzzle compilers and authors of many books, for their enthusiasm in the field of IQ testing and puzzles.

Culture-Free Section

The modern thinking on IQ tests is that the most reliable are culture free, where no prior knowledge or skill with words is necessary. A culture-free test breaks down all language barriers. Such tests are truly international and can be applied to all people, irrespective of creed and culture.

All the tests in this section consist entirely of diagrammatic representation. To solve them you must apply your mind to each set of diagrams, comprehend the experience before you, and decide what logical patterns and/or sequences are occurring. These tests are purely exercises of the mind, designed to test raw intelligence, free from the influence of prior knowledge.

In this section are four separate tests. Each test contains twenty questions and you are allowed a time of forty minutes to complete the twenty questions. Study the instructions for each question and select which you think is the correct answer from the choices given. You should keep strictly to the time limit as any delay could invalidate your score. Work as quickly as possible, not spending too much time on any one question; if in doubt leave it and return to it, using any time remaining. If necessary have an intuitive guess — which may well be the correct answer.

Answers are given at the end of each test, but do not look at these until you have finished the whole test, in case you inadvertently read the solution to the next puzzle.

CULTURE-FREE

Test
1

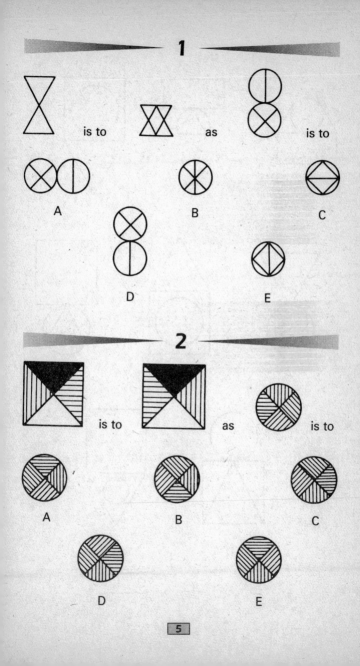

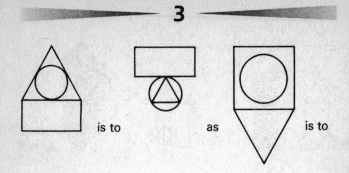

is to   as   is to

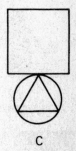

A   B   C

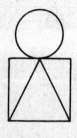

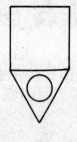

D   E

 is to as is to

A

B

C

D

E

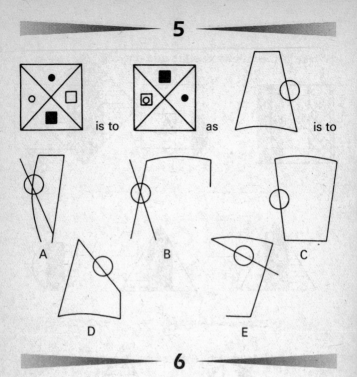

is to ... as ... is to

Which of the following is the odd one out?

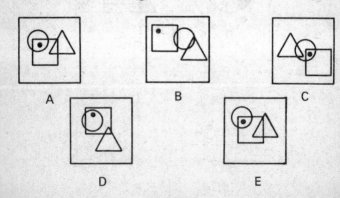

Which of the following is the odd one out?

A B C

D E

Which of the following is the odd one out?

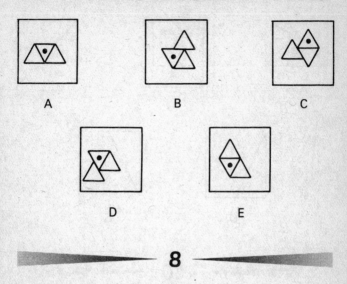

A B C

D E

Which of the following is the odd one out?

A

B

C

D

E

Which of the following is the odd one out?

A

B

C

D

E

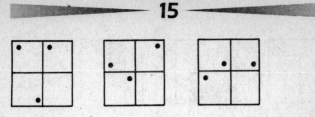

Which of the following continues the sequence above?

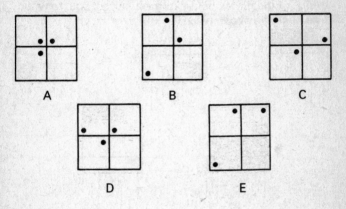

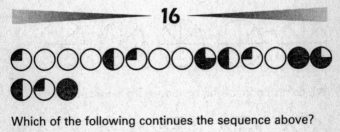

Which of the following continues the sequence above?

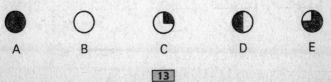

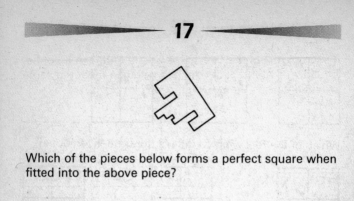

Which of the pieces below forms a perfect square when fitted into the above piece?

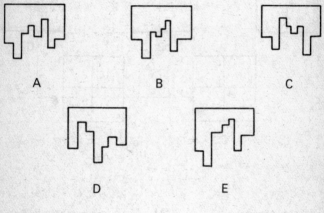

A

B

C

D

E

To which one of the five boxes on the right can a dot be added so that the dot in the box will then meet the same conditions as in the box on the left?

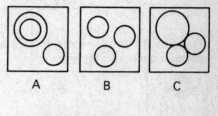

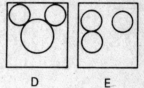

To which one of the five boxes on the right can a dot be
added so that the dots in the box will then meet the same
conditions as in the box on the left?

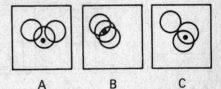

A   B   C

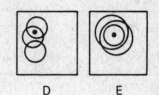

D   E

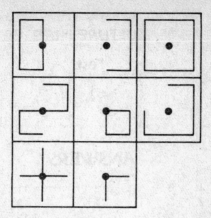

Look along each horizontal line and then down each vertical line to decide which should logically be the missing square.

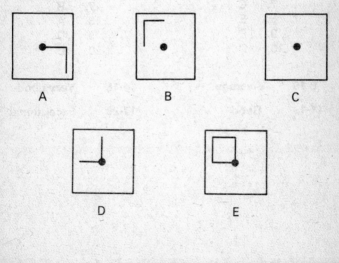

A

B

C

D

E

CULTURE FREE

Test

1

ANSWERS

1.	B	11.	B
2.	D	12.	C
3.	A	13.	D
4.	B	14.	E
5.	B	15.	B
6.	B	16.	A
7.	C	17.	B
8.	E	18.	A
9.	E	19.	D
10.	D	20.	C

8-10	Average	14-16	Very good
11-13	Good	17-20	Exceptional

CULTURE-FREE

Test
2

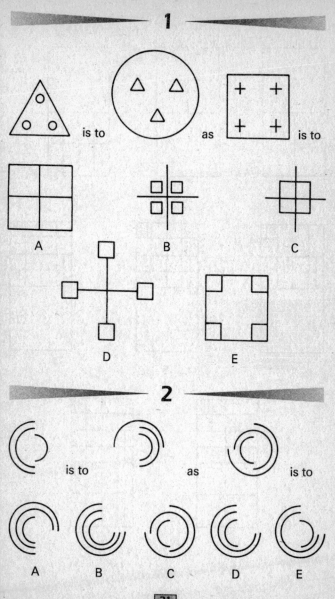

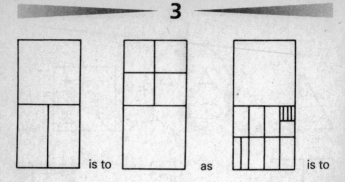

is to ... as ... is to

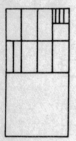

A

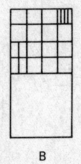

B

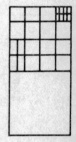

C

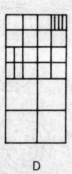

D

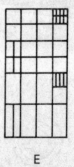

E

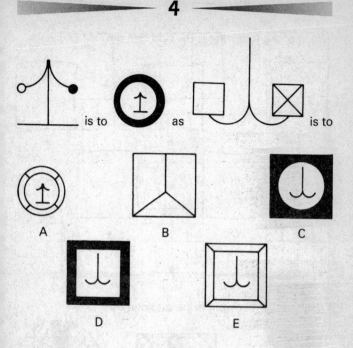

is to ... as ... is to

A
B
C

D
E

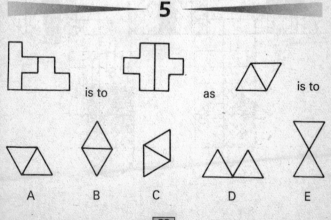

is to ... as ... is to

A
B
C
D
E

Which of the following is the odd one out?

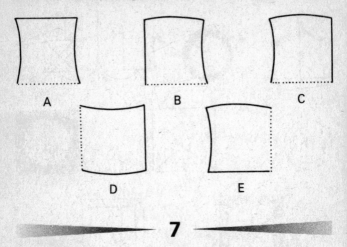

A   B   C

D   E

Which of the following is the odd one out?

 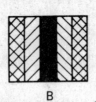 

A   B   C

D

E

Which of the following is the odd one out?

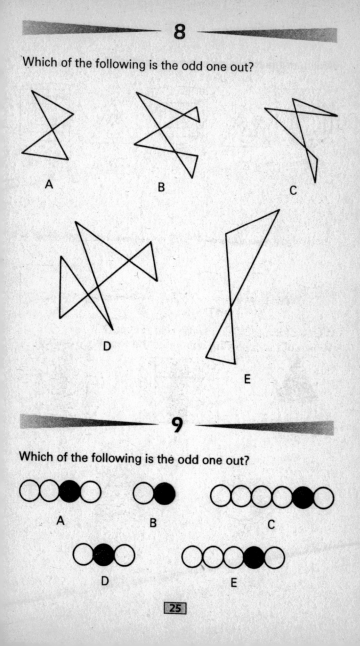

A

B

C

D

E

Which of the following is the odd one out?

A

B

C

D

E

Which of the following is the odd one out?

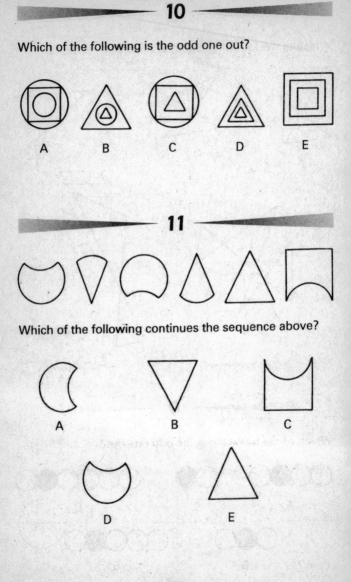

A   B   C   D   E

Which of the following continues the sequence above?

A   B   C

D   E

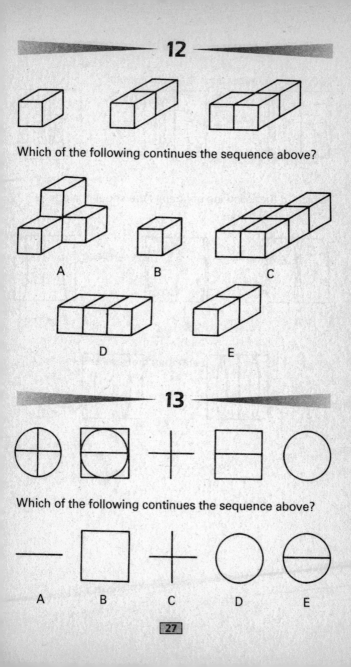

Which of the following continues the sequence above?

A B C

D E

Which of the following continues the sequence above?

A B C D E

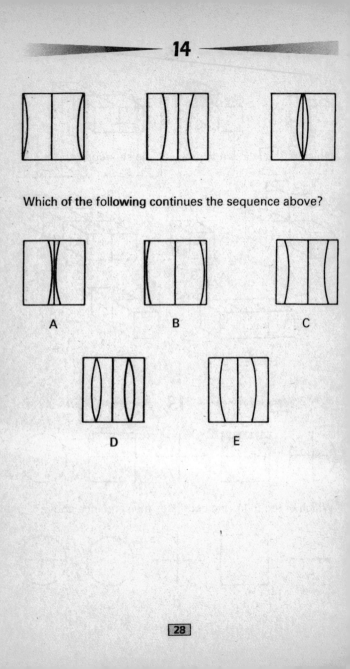

Which of the following continues the sequence above?

A

B

C

D

E

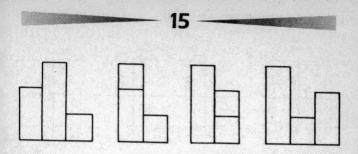

Which of the following continues the sequence above?

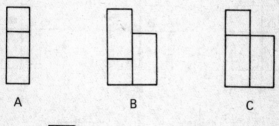

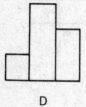

A

B

C

D

E

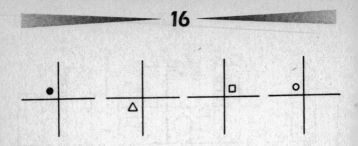

Which of the following continues the sequence above?

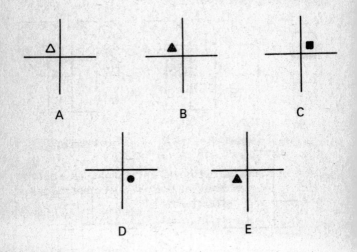

A   B   C

D   E

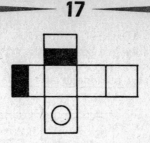

When the above is folded to form a cube, how many of
the following can be produced?

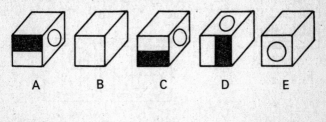

A   B   C   D   E

To which one of the five boxes on the right can a dot be
added so that the dot in the box will then meet the same
conditions as in the box on the left?

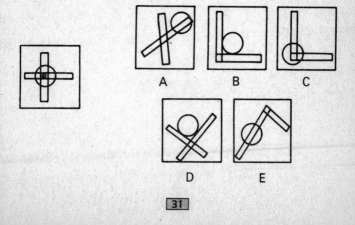

A   B   C

D   E

To which one of the five boxes on the right can a dot be added so that the dots in the box will then meet the same conditions as in the box on the left?

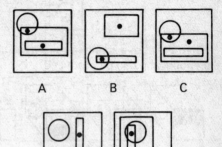

A B C

D E

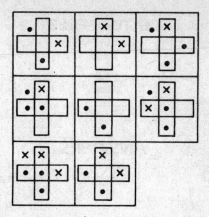

Look along each horizontal line and then down each vertical line to decide which logically should be the missing square.

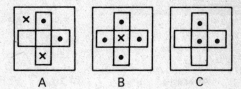

A   B   C

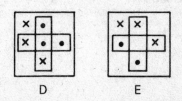

D   E

CULTURE-FREE

Test
2

ANSWERS

1.	B	11.	B	
2.	D	12.	A	
3.	C	13.	D	
4.	E	14.	E	
5.	A	15.	B	
6.	A	16.	E	
7.	D.	17.	C, D, E	
8.	C	18.	C	
9.	B	19.	B	
10.	C	20.	D	

8-10	Average	14-16	Very good
11-13	Good	17-20	Exceptional

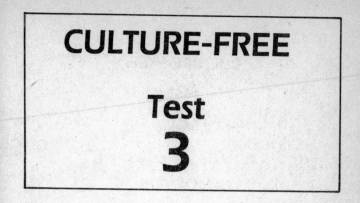

CULTURE-FREE

Test

3

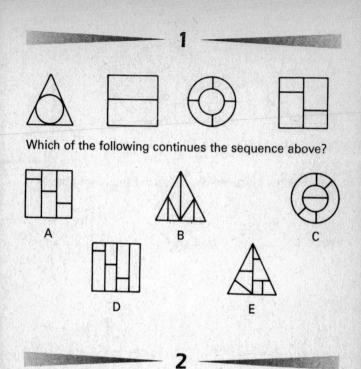

Which of the following continues the sequence above?

A

B

C

D

E

Which of the following is the odd one out?

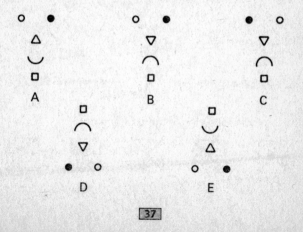

A

B

C

D

E

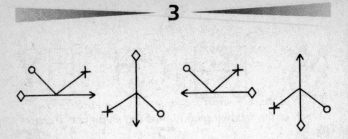

Which of the following continues the sequence above?

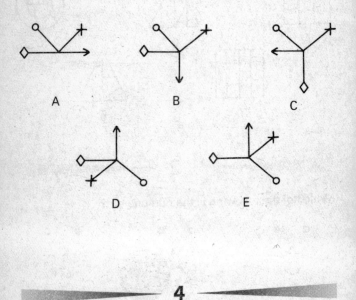

A

B

C

D

E

Which of the following is the odd one out?

A　　　　B　　　　C　　　　D　　　　E

N F H Y

Which of the following continues the sequence above?

M E Z L T

A   B   C   D   E

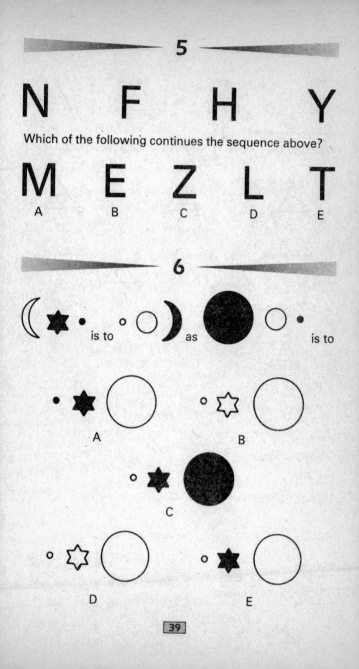

is to ... as ... is to

A

B

C

D

E

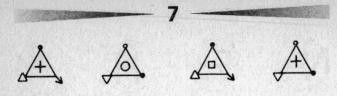

Which of the following continues the sequence above?

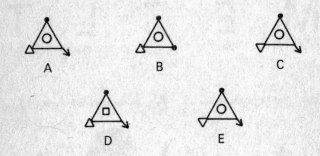

A   B   C

D   E

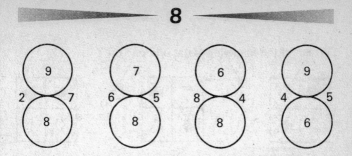

Which of the following continues the sequence above?

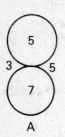

A

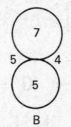

B

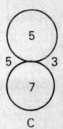

C

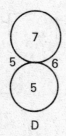

D

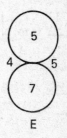

E

Which of the following is the odd one out?

A

B

C

D

E

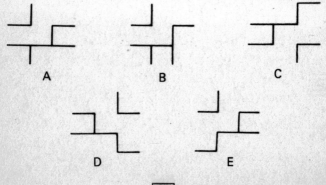

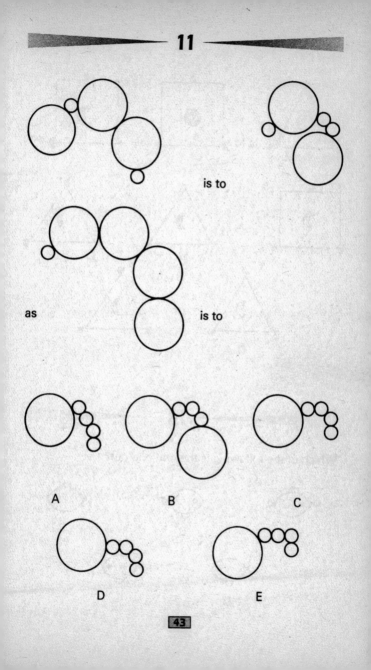

is to

as

is to

A

B

C

D

E

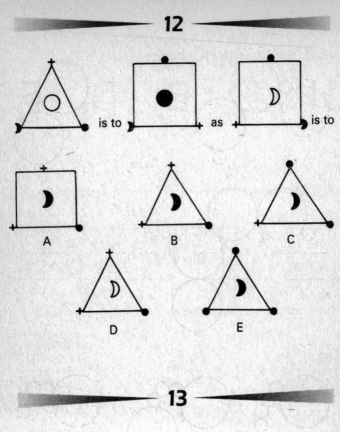

is to ... as ... is to

A B C

D E

Which of the following is the odd one out?

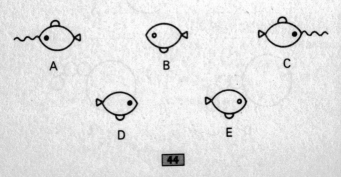

A B C

D E

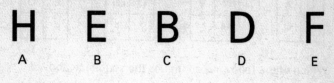

14

Which of the following is the odd one out?

H   **E**   **B**   **D**   **F**

A   B   C   D   E

15

4	1
8	12

9	6
13	27

16	13
20	48

25	22
29	75

Which of the following continues the sequence above?

35	33
40	108

A

36	33
40	107

B

36	33
40	108

C

36	32
40	108

D

36	33
39	108

E

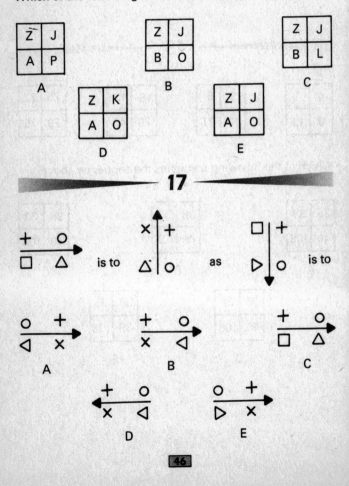

L	X
O	A

N	V
M	C

Q	S
J	F

U	O
F	J

Which of the following continues the sequence above?

Z̃	J
A	P

A

Z	J
B	O

B

Z	J
B	L

C

Z	K
A	O

D

Z	J
A	O

E

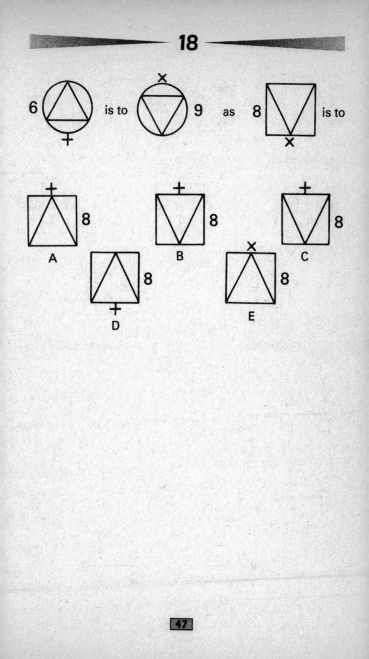

is to

as

is to

A

B

C

D

E

is to ⬚ as ⬚ is to

A   B   C   D   E

CULTURE-FREE

Test
3

ANSWERS

1.	B		11.	C
2.	B		12.	B
3.	A		13.	D
4.	B		14.	E
5.	C		15.	E
6.	E		16.	E
7.	A		17.	C
8.	C		18.	A
9.	C		19.	C
10.	E		20.	A

8-10	Average	14-16	Very good
11-13	Good	17-20	Exceptional

CULTURE-FREE

Test
4

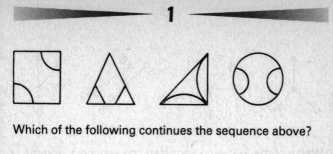

Which of the following continues the sequence above?

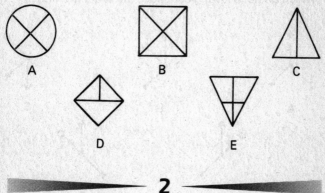

A

B

C

D

E

Which of the following is the odd one out?

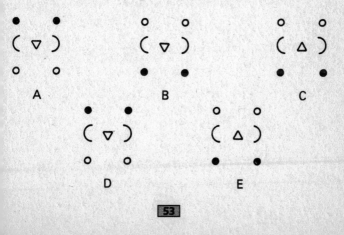

A

B

C

D

E

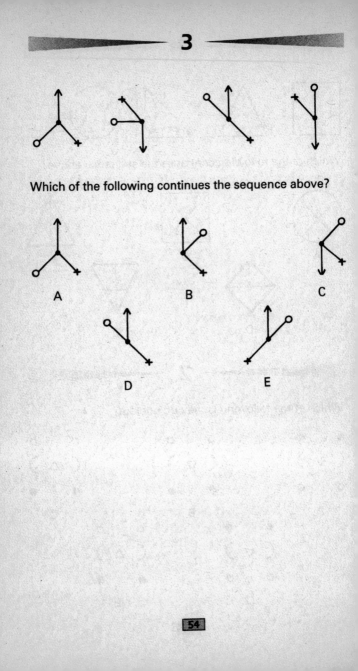

Which of the following continues the sequence above?

A

B

C

D

E

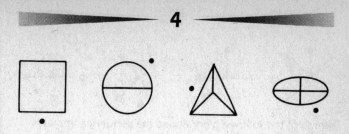

Which of the following continues the sequence above?

A

B

C

D

E

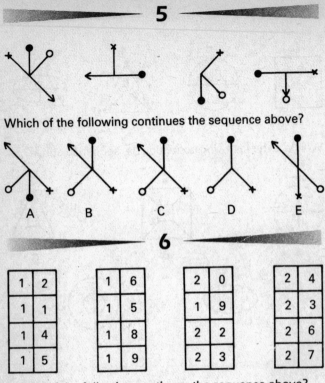

Which of the following continues the sequence above?

A   B   C   D   E

1	2
1	1
1	4
1	5

1	6
1	5
1	8
1	9

2	0
1	9
2	2
2	3

2	4
2	3
2	6
2	7

Which of the following continues the sequence above?

2	8
2	9
3	0
3	1

A

2	8
2	7
3	0
3	0

B

2	8
2	7
3	0
3	1

C

2	8
2	7
2	9
3	1

D

2	8
2	7
3	0
3	0

E

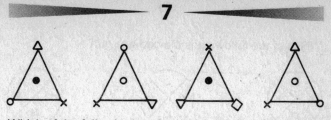

Which of the following continues the sequence above?

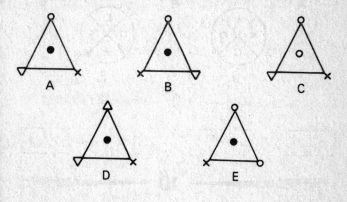

What number should be placed at ?

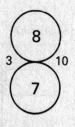 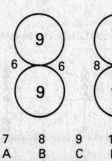 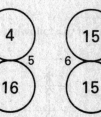

7	8	9	10	11
A	B	C	D	E

Which of the following is the odd one out?

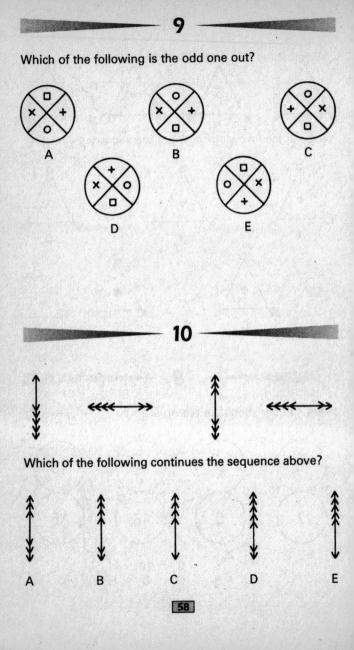

A

B

C

D

E

Which of the following continues the sequence above?

A   B   C   D   E

Which of the following is the odd one out?

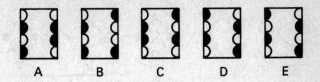

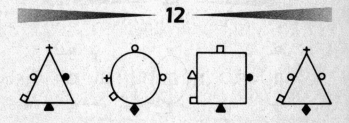

Which of the following continues the sequence above?

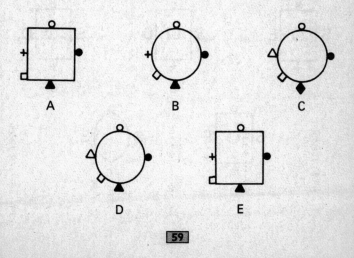

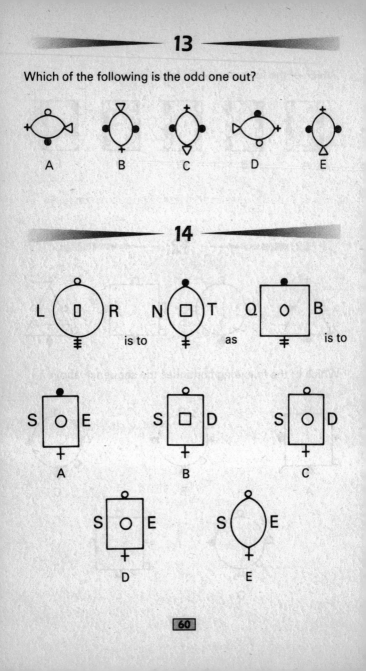

Which of the following is the odd one out?

A   B   C   D   E

L ▢ R   N ▢ T   Q ○ B

is to   as   is to

S ○ E   S ▢ D   S ○ D
A   B   C

S ○ E   S ○ E
D   E

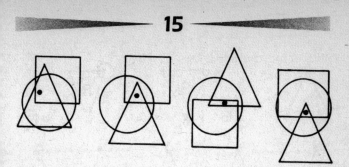

Which of the following continues the sequence above?

A   B   C

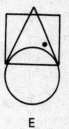

D   E

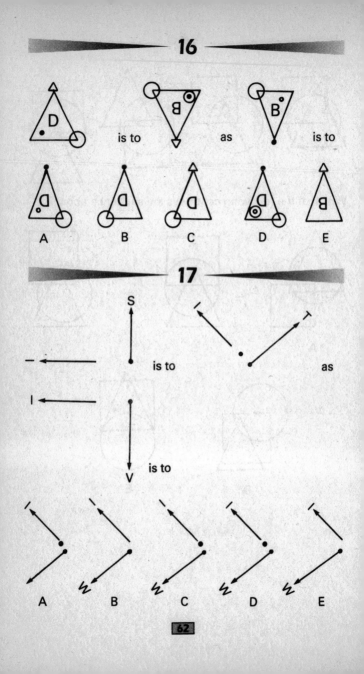

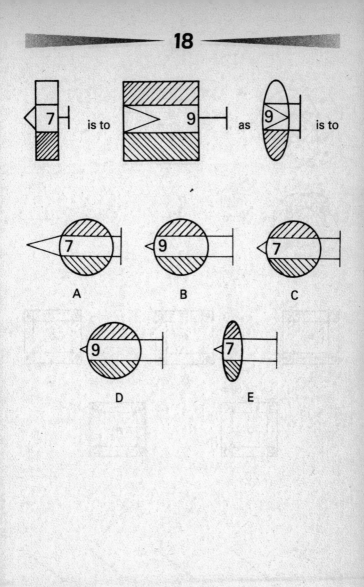

is to ... as ... is to

A   B   C

D   E

is to as

 is to

A

B   C

D

E

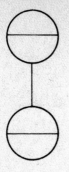 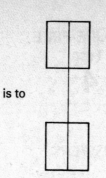 is to 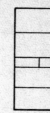 as 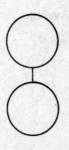 is to

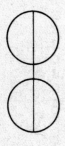

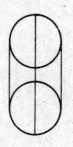

A

B

C

D

E

CULTURE-FREE
Test
4

ANSWERS

1.	D		11.	B
2.	B		12.	B
3.	B		13.	C
4.	B		14.	C
5.	C		15.	B
6.	B		16.	D
7.	A		17.	C
8.	D		18.	C
9.	B		19.	C
10.	E		20.	B

8-10	**Average**	**14-16**	**Very good**
11-13	**Good**	**17-20**	**Exceptional**

Industrial Section

This section is designed to test your scientific and technical knowledge in a wide range of subjects, to determine how far you have applied your intelligence in building up a store of knowledge of a general nature.

This section consists of four separate tests of twenty questions each. You are allowed a time of sixty minutes to complete each set of twenty questions. Most questions are accompanied by an illustration or diagram with a choice of answers. You must select the correct answer using a mixture of *knowledge, reasoning* and *intuition*. You should keep strictly to the time limit as any delay could invalidate your score. Calculators must not be used but you are allowed to work out on paper any calculations you think are necessary.

Work as quickly as possible, not spending too much time on any one question; if in doubt leave it and return to it using any time remaining. Remember that this section is also designed to test your powers of reasoning and intuition, so if necessary have an intuitive guess as this may well be the correct answer.

Answers are given at the end of each test, but do not look at these until you have finished the whole test, in case you inadvertently read the solution to the next puzzle.

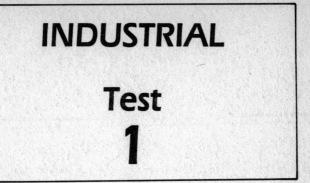

INDUSTRIAL

Test
1

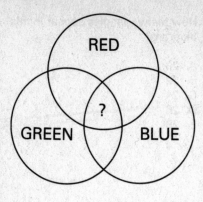

Three coloured lights — red, green and blue — are projected on to a screen. What is the new colour produced when all three colours merge in the centre?

A. White
B. Black
C. Yellow
D. Purple
E. Grey

The value of each angle in a square is 90°. What is the value of each angle in a hexagon?

A. 108°
B. 120°
C. 135°
D. 140°
E. 150°

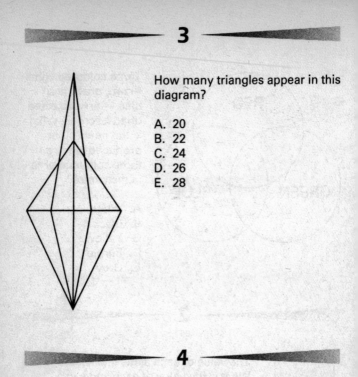

How many triangles appear in this diagram?

A. 20
B. 22
C. 24
D. 26
E. 28

5 !

Does the mathematical sign (!) mean:

A. $5 \times 5 \times 5 \times 5 \times 5$
B. 5.555 to infinity
C. .555 to infinity
D. $5 \times 4 \times 3 \times 2 \times 1$
E. $(5 \times 5) + (5 \times 5) + (5 \times 5) + (5 \times 5) + (5 \times 5)$?

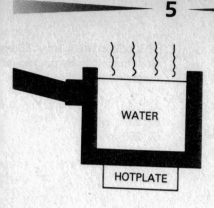

By what method is heat transferred from the hotplate to the water?

A. Radiation
B. Conduction
C. Thermal
D. Convection
E. Molecular

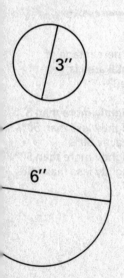

If the diameter of a pipe is doubled, does this increase its capacity by:

A. 2
B. 3
C. 3.1416
D. 4
E. 8?

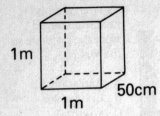

1m

50cm

1m

This box is 1m × 1m × 50cm.
How many can be packed into
container 9m × 5m × 3m?

A. 135
B. 202
C. 250
D. 270
E. 337

What percentage of
the total area is
shaded?

A. Slightly more than 33%
B. Slightly less than 50%
C. Exactly 50%
D. Slightly more than 50%
E. Slightly less than 66%

What type of knot is shown here?

A. Bowline
B. Clove hitch
C. Single sheet bend
D. Reef
E. Sheep shank

In Morse code, what letter is represented by these three dots?

A. R
B. S
C. T
D. U
E. V

What tune is this the first line of?

A. Happy Birthday
B. The French National Anthem
C. The British National Anthem
D. The American National Anthem
E. God Bless America

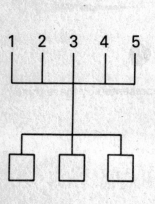

Any three of the numbers 1-5 can be placed in the three boxes provided at any one time, but the same number cannot be used twice in any one operation (i.e. 412 is possible but 442 is not). How many different three figure numbers can be formed?

A. 20
B. 50
C. 60
D. 100
E. 120

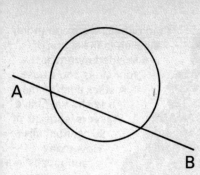

What is the name of
the line AB?

A. Segment
B. Chord
C. Radius
D. Tangent
E. Secant

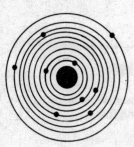

Of the nine major planets which
is the smallest?

A. Earth
B. Mars
C. Mercury
D. Pluto
E. Neptune

Cannonballs were commonly stacked in the shape of five sided pyramids, i.e. four sides and a base. A stack such as the one shown, of five layers, consists of 55 cannonballs. How many cannonballs in a seven layer pyramid?

A. 91
B. 120
C. 140
D. 182
E. 204

If two dice are thrown, what is the possibility of scoring five?

A. 1/12
B. 1/9
C. 1/6
D. 1/15
E. 1/18

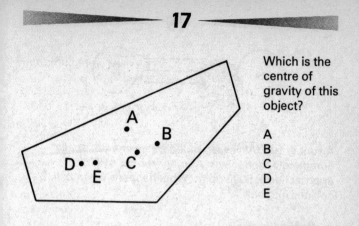

Which is the centre of gravity of this object?

A
B
C
D
E

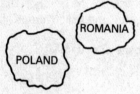

Which country has the largest land mass?

A. Romania
B. Poland
C. Yugoslavia
D. United Kingdom
E. West Germany

(Drawn to scale)

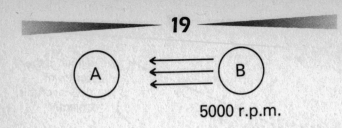

5000 r.p.m.

A rubber ball 'A' is suspended freely in outer space completely motionless. Another rubber ball 'B' approaches at 5000 r.p.m. What happens when ball 'B' collides into ball 'A'?

A. Both balls disintegrate
B. Both balls shoot off in opposite directions at 2500 r.p.m.
C. Both balls shoot off in the same direction at 2500 r.p.m.
D. Ball 'A' shoots off at 5000 r.p.m. and ball 'B' stops motionless
E. Both balls shoot off in opposite directions at 5000 r.p.m.

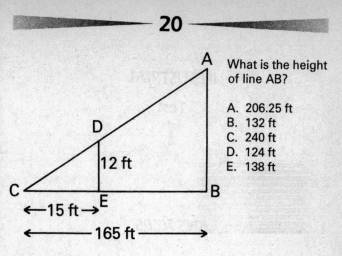

What is the height of line AB?

A. 206.25 ft
B. 132 ft
C. 240 ft
D. 124 ft
E. 138 ft

A

D

12 ft

C

E

B

←15 ft→

←———— 165 ft ————→

(Not to scale)

INDUSTRIAL

Test
1

ANSWERS

1.	A		11.	C
2.	B		12.	C
3.	C		13.	E
4.	D		14.	C
5.	B		15.	C
6.	D		16.	B
7.	D		17.	C
8.	B		18.	B
9.	D		19.	D
10.	B		20.	B

8-10	Average	14-16	Very good
11-13	Good	17-20	Exceptional

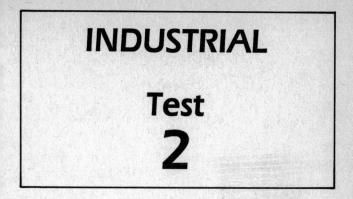

INDUSTRIAL

Test
2

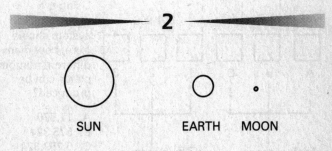

If you fold this piece of card along the lines to form a regular solid (all surfaces of equal size), what will its name be?

A. Tetrahedron
B. Hexahedron
C. Octahedron
D. Dodecahedron
E. Icosahedron

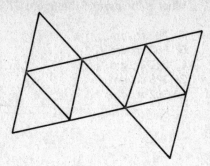

SUN   EARTH   MOON

(Not to scale)

Is this a,

A. Total eclipse of the sun
B. Partial eclipse of the sun
C. Annular eclipse of the sun
D. Total eclipse of the moon
E. Partial eclipse of the moon?

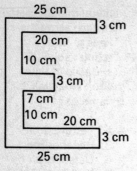

25 cm

3 cm

20 cm

10 cm

3 cm

7 cm

10 cm   20 cm

3 cm

25 cm

(*Not to scale*)

What is the area of the figure E?

A. 262 sq. cm.
B. 286 sq. cm.
C. 312 sq. cm.
D. 328 sq. cm.
E. 352 sq. cm.

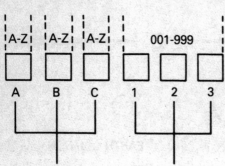

| A-Z | A-Z | A-Z | | 001-999 | |
| A | B | C | 1 | 2 | 3 |

Each of these three spaces can contain one of the 26 letters of the alphabet

The numbers 001-999 appear in these three spaces

Using the number plate system shown here, how many different number plates can be produced?

A. 17,576
B. 675,324
C. 6,759,324
D. 17,558,424
E. 25,785,576

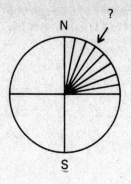

Which point of the compass is indicated by the arrow?

A. NW by N
B. NNE
C. NE by N
D. NE by E
E. N by E

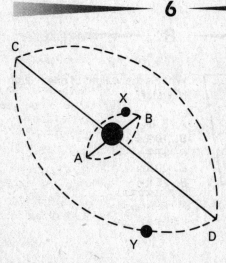

The orbits of two planets X and Y are shown around the sun. Line CD is four times that of line AB. If planet X takes one year to go round the sun, how long does planet Y take?

A. 2 years
B. 3 years
C. 4 years
D. 6 years
E. 8 years

To find the surface area of a ball do you multiply the square of the diameter by,

A. 2
B. 3.5
C. 3.1416
D. 3.3927
E. 5.6?

What is the weight of one gallon of water?

A. 5 lbs
B. 10 lbs
C. 15 lbs
D. 20 lbs
E. 25 lbs

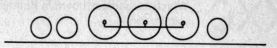

What wheel arrangement is shown here?

A. 2-3-1
B. 4-3-2
C. 4-6-2
D. 4-6-1
E. 2-3-2

How many squares, including the one large square, are to be found in the diagram?

A. 29
B. 30
C. 31
D. 32
E. 33

XXC

Which number is shown in Roman numerals?

A. 80
B. 120
C. 900
D. 200
E. 10,000

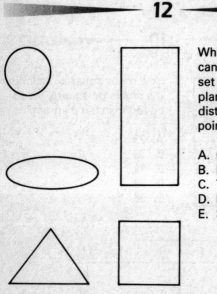

Which of these figures can be described as 'a set of all points in a plane at a fixed distance from a fixed point in the plane'?

A. Circle
B. Ellipse
C. Triangle
D. Rectangle
E. Square

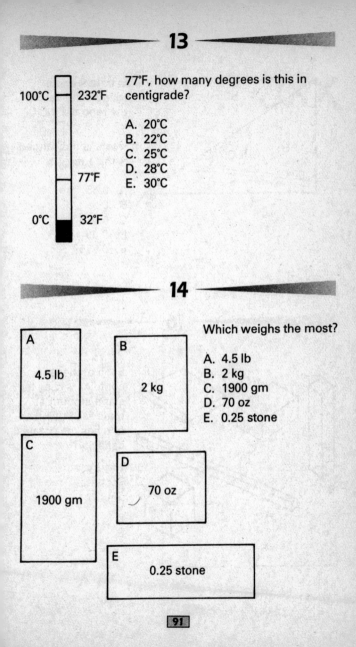

77°F, how many degrees is this in centigrade?

100°C — 232°F

77°F

0°C — 32°F

A. 20°C
B. 22°C
C. 25°C
D. 28°C
E. 30°C

Which weighs the most?

A. 4.5 lb
B. 2 kg
C. 1900 gm
D. 70 oz
E. 0.25 stone

A 4.5 lb

B 2 kg

C 1900 gm

D 70 oz

E 0.25 stone

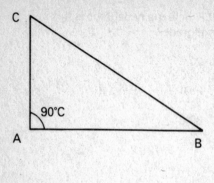

In a right-angled triangle the value of the ratio of LINE CA

LINE BA

remains unchanged. Is this ratio,

A. 0.55
B. 0.6
C. 0.625
D. 0.65
E. 0.675?

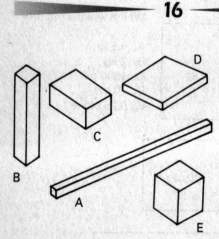

Each of these containers uses the same amount of material, but which one has the greatest capacity?

A
B
C
D
E

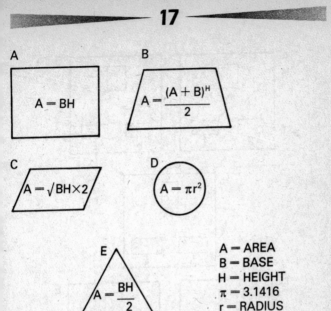

A

$A = BH$

B

$A = \dfrac{(A + B)^H}{2}$

C

$A = \sqrt{BH} \times 2$

D

$A = \pi r^2$

E

$A = \dfrac{BH}{2}$

A = AREA
B = BASE
H = HEIGHT
π = 3.1416
r = RADIUS

Written within each of the shapes is the formula for finding their area. Which one is incorrect?

A. Rectangle
B. Trapezium
C. Parallelogram
D. Circle
E. Triangle

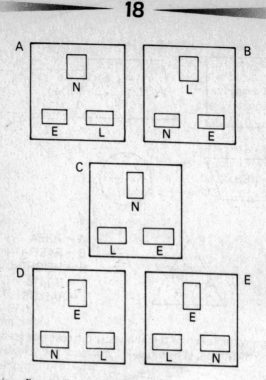

Of these five wall plug sockets only one has the correct hole markings. Is it,

A. Neutral-Earth-Live
B. Live-Neutral-Earth
C. Neutral-Live-Earth
D. Earth-Neutral-Live
E. Earth-Live-Neutral?

Tetrahedrons are shapes with four surfaces, i.e. a three-sided triangle with base. The number of balls stacked in such a shape are called tetrahedral numbers, e.g. ten balls are required for a three-tier pyramid, as illustrated.
How many balls would be required for a five-tier pyramid?

A. 20
B. 25
C. 30
D. 35
E. 40

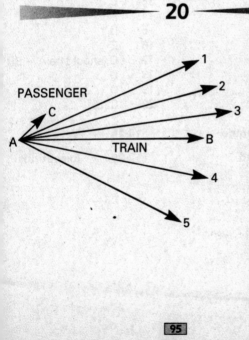

PASSENGER

TRAIN

A train is moving in the direction AB and a passenger on the train walks from one side of the compartment to the other in the direction AC. In what direction is he actually moving relative to the earth?

A. 1
B. 2
C. 3
D. 4
E. 5

INDUSTRIAL

Test
2

ANSWERS

1.	C		11.	A
2.	D		12.	A
3.	B		13.	C
4.	D		14.	A
5.	C		15.	B
6.	E		16.	E
7.	C		17.	C (should be A = BH)
8.	B		18.	D
9.	C		19.	D
10.	B		20.	C (3)

8-10	**Average**	**14-16**	**Very good**
11-13	**Good**	**17-20**	**Exceptional**

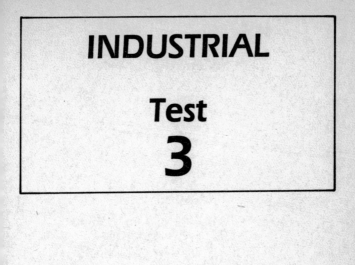

INDUSTRIAL

Test
3

An aeroplane flies due south at 500 m.p.h. There is a wind blowing at 100 m.p.h. from the SE. Which direction will the aeroplane have to fly in, in order to arrive at the correct destination, and at what speed to arrive at the correct time?

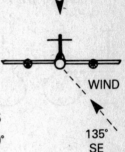

180°
SOUTH
500 m.p.h.

WIND

135°
SE
100 m.p.h.

	A	B	C	D	E
Speed m.p.h.	575	425	500	575	425
Direction	190°	190°	180°	170°	170°

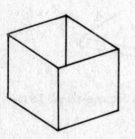

If you wanted to make a square-based water tank out of sheet metal, without a lid, how would you make it in order to use the least amount of metal sheet for the greatest possible volume?

A. Square base with sides same height as base
B. Square base with sides twice height of base
C. Square base with sides half height of base
D. Square base with sides three times height of base
E. None of these

In Greece, in ancient times, potters made jugs in a shape which was pleasant to the human eye and had the most pleasing proportions. This is the Golden Section.
What proportion is x of the whole?

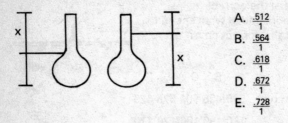

A. $\frac{.512}{1}$

B. $\frac{.564}{1}$

C. $\frac{.618}{1}$

D. $\frac{.672}{1}$

E. $\frac{.728}{1}$

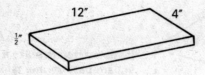

What is the weight of this piece of flat steel plate? To the nearest lb.

A. 14 lbs

B. 6 lbs

C. 18 lbs

D. 10 lbs

E. 12 lbs

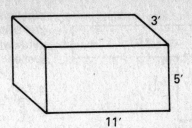

How many Petrograd Standards in this stack of timber?

A. 1
B. 2
C. 3
D. 4
E. 5

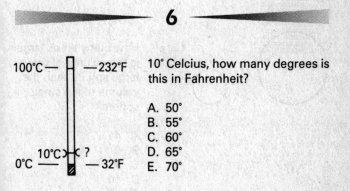

10° Celcius, how many degrees is this in Fahrenheit?

A. 50°
B. 55°
C. 60°
D. 65°
E. 70°

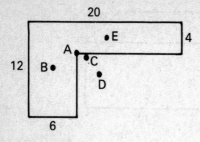

Where is the centre of gravity of this plate of metal when suspended flat?

Is it A
B
C
D
E?

How many times larger is the volume of the large sphere than the volume of the small sphere?

A 4
B 6
C 8
D 10
E 12

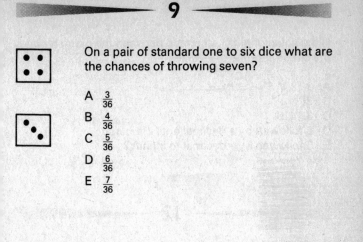

On a pair of standard one to six dice what are the chances of throwing seven?

A $\frac{3}{36}$

B $\frac{4}{36}$

C $\frac{5}{36}$

D $\frac{6}{36}$

E $\frac{7}{36}$

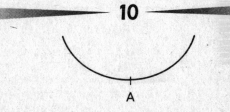

A

A curve, on which a ball, placed anywhere on the inner surface, will always take the same time to arrive at point A when allowed to roll down, is called a

A Hyperbolic curve
B Catenary curve
C Parabolic curve
D Conic curve
E Cardioid curve?

11

Is the value of pi (π), (the ratio between the diameter and the circumference of a circle)

A 3
B $3\frac{1}{7}$
C 3.1416
D 3 followed by a decimal until it recurs
E 3 followed by a decimal to infinity?

12

The Fibonacci series goes:

0   1   1   2   3   5   8   13   21   34   55   etc.

What is the seventeenth term?

A 610
B 877
C 987
D 1364
E 1597

13

What is the size of a normal house brick?

A 215mm × 102.5mm × 102.5mm
B 215mm × 102.5mm × 65mm
C 415mm × 102.5mm × 102.5mm
D 415mm × 215mm × 102.5mm
E 615mm × 215mm × 215mm

On a piano keyboard which key is C?

1
2
3
4
5

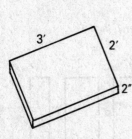

Concrete paving stones weigh 144 lbs per cubic foot.
How many would you get from a ton?

A 9-11
B 11-13
C 13-15
D 15-17
E 17-19

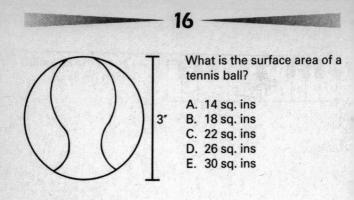

What is the surface area of a
tennis ball?

A. 14 sq. ins
B. 18 sq. ins
C. 22 sq. ins
D. 26 sq. ins
E. 30 sq. ins

Which is the strongest timber beam?

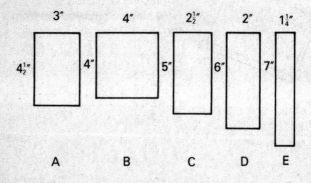

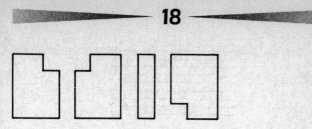

A tiler wished to display some tiles so cut six for his display. Here are the first four tiles.

Which of the following five are the last two?

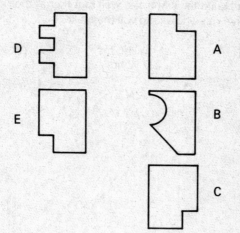

One bricklayer can build a wall in 3 hours.
One bricklayer can build a wall in 4 hours.
One bricklayer can build a wall in 5 hours.
One bricklayer can build a wall in 6 hours.

If they all build the same size wall together at their respective rates how long will they take?

A ½ hr
B 1 hr
C 1½ hrs
D 2 hrs
E 2½ hrs

Which two man-hole covers are safer?

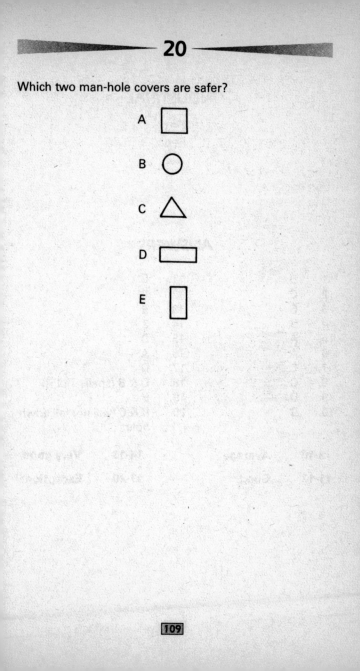

A

B

C

D

E

INDUSTRIAL

Test
3

ANSWERS

1.	D	11.	E
2.	C	12.	C
3.	C	13.	B
4.	B	14.	3
5.	A	15.	D
6.	A	16.	A
7.	C	17.	D
8.	C	18.	D & B (spells TILER)
9.	D	19.	B
10.	B	20.	B & C (will not fall down hole)

8-10	Average	14-16	Very good
11-13	Good	17-20	Exceptional

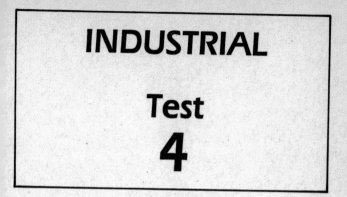

INDUSTRIAL

Test
4

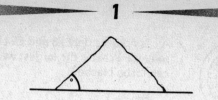

If dry sand is allowed to fall into a pile freely it will form a cone shape. This angle is called the angle of repose, what is the angle?

A. 25°
B. 33°
C. 40°
D. 45°
E. 50°

2

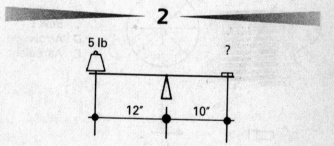

What value weight must be placed in the pan to balance the scale?

A. 4 lb
B. 5 lb
C. 6 lb
D. 7 lb
E. 8 lb

A casino uses only £8 and £5 chips at roulette. What is the largest wager that *cannot* be placed?

A. £23
B. £27
C. £59
D. £717
E. £1023

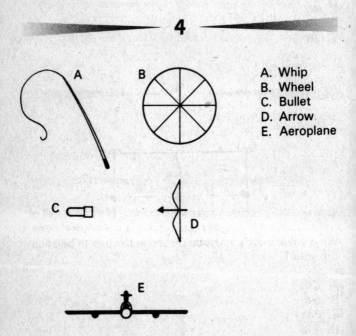

A. Whip
B. Wheel
C. Bullet
D. Arrow
E. Aeroplane

What was the earliest man-made artifact that broke the sound barrier?

How many sides do snowflakes have?

A. 4
B. 5
C. 6
D. 8
E. Varies

Which sport has a night-watchman and a third man?

A. Ice-hockey
B. Soccer
C. Basketball
D. Cricket
E. Volley-ball

What are the chances of drawing the ace of spades out of a pack of fifty-two playing cards, then in the second draw, taking out the ace of hearts?

A. $\frac{1}{896}$

B. $\frac{1}{1266}$

C. $\frac{1}{1826}$

D. $\frac{1}{2652}$

E. $\frac{1}{3892}$

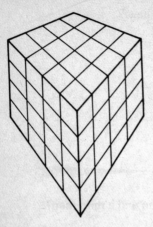

8

Sixty-four cube bricks are stacked and painted on the five exposed sides.
During the night the wind scatters the bricks, you pick up one at random, what are the chances of selecting a brick which is unpainted on all six faces?

A. $\frac{10}{64}$ D. $\frac{16}{24}$

B. $\frac{12}{64}$ E. $\frac{18}{64}$

C. $\frac{14}{64}$

9

HORSE-RACING
4.00 Everingham Maiden Stakes

		Odds
1	Anfield's Star	5-2
2	Fresh from Victory	7-2
3	James Star	9-2
4	King of Sailors	5-1
5	Lapiaffe	10-1
6	Mariner's Law	16-1
7	Turture	20-1
8	Dayadari	?

What odds should the bookmaker give on Dayadari to give himself a ten per cent margin on the race, assuming that he balanced his books?

A. 20-1   D. 40-1
B. 25-1   E. 50-1
C. 30-1

On a pair of eight-sided dice what are the chances of throwing at least twelve?

A. $\frac{14}{64}$

B. $\frac{15}{64}$

C. $\frac{16}{64}$

D. $\frac{17}{64}$

E. $\frac{18}{64}$

What is the volume of the ice-cream cone?

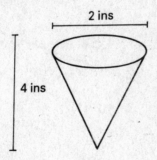

2 ins

4 ins

A. 10 c.ins
B. 12 c.ins
C. 14 c.ins
D. 16 c.ins
E. 18 c.ins

A man has a cask of 100 pints of wine and a cask of 100 pints of water. He takes a pint of wine out of the wine cask and puts it into the water cask, then he takes a pint of water and wine mixed out of the water cask and puts it into the wine cask. Is there more wine in the water cask than water in the wine cask?

A. $\frac{1}{101}$ pints more wine

B. $\frac{100}{101}$ pints more wine

C. Same

D. $\frac{1}{101}$ pints less wine

E. $\frac{100}{101}$ pints less wine

The following dice game is very popular at fairs and carnivals, but since two persons seldom agree on the chances of a player winning, I offer it as an elementary problem in the theory of probability.

On the counter are six squares marked 1, 2, 3, 4, 5, 6. Players are invited to place as much money as they wish on any one square. Three dice are then thrown. If your number appears on one die only, you get your money back plus the same amount. If two dice show your number, you get your money back plus twice the amount you placed on the square. If your number appears on all three dice, you get your money back plus three times the amount. Of course if the number is not on any of the dice, the operator gets your money.

A player might reason: the chance of my number showing on one die is 1/6, but since there are three dice, the chances must be 3/6 or 1/2, therefore the game is a fair one. Of course this is the way the operator of the game wants everyone to reason, for it is quite fallacious.

Is the game favourable to the operator or the player, and in either case, just how favourable is it?

Out of 216 possible ways the dice may be thrown do you win on

A. 81
B. 91
C. 101
D. 111
E. 121?

While the property boom was on, a developer stopped
off at a wrong station and, having a couple of hours to
wait for the next train, made a quick and profitable deal.
He bought a piece of land for £243 which he divided into
equal lots, then sold them at £18 per lot, cleaning up the
whole transaction before his train arrived. His profit on
the deal was exactly equal to what six of the lots
originally cost him.

How many lots were in that piece of land?

A. 15
B. 16
C. 17
D. 18
E. 19

If an elastic ball is dropped from the Leaning Tower of
Pisa from a height of 179 feet from the ground, and on
each rebound the ball rises exactly one tenth of its
previous height, what distance will it travel before it
comes to rest?

A. 214 ft
B. 218 ft
C. 222 ft
D. 226 ft
E. 230 ft

While enjoying a giddy ride on the carousel, Bobby propounded this problem: 'One-third of the number of kids riding ahead of me, added to three-quarters of those riding behind me, gives the correct number of children on this merry-go-round.'
How many children were riding the carousel?

A. 10
B. 11
C. 12
D. 13
E. 14

Sally explained to Elizabeth that she has a larger square cabbage patch now than she had last year and will therefore raise 211 more cabbages. How many cabbages will Sally raise this year?

A. 7934
B. 8216
C. 9874
D. 11,236
E. 13,186

A Texas ranchman, who owned more land than he could conveniently farm, leased half of a certain field to a neighbour. This field was 2,000 yards long by 1,000 yards wide, but because of certain bad streaks which ran through the land it was decided that a fairer division would be obtained by cutting a band around the field than by dividing it in half.

What is the width of a border strip, to be cut all round that field, that will contain exactly half of the total crop? There is a simple rule which will apply to any rectangular field.

A. 191 yds
B. 192 yds
C. 193 yds
D. 194 yds
E. 195 yds

According to Mother Goose, Jack Spratt could eat no fat and his wife could eat no lean.

Together they could eat a barrel of fat pork in sixty days, whereas it would take Jack thirty weeks to perform this feat alone.

Together they could consume a barrel of lean pork in eight weeks, although his wife alone could not dispose of it in less than forty weeks.

Assuming that Jack would always eat lean pork whenever it was available and that his wife would do the same with fat, how long would it take both of them to eat a barrel of mixed pork, half fat and half lean?

A. 30 days
B. 35 days
C. 40 days
D. 45 days
E. 50 days

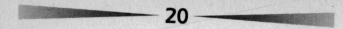

Three Texas drovers met on the highway and proceeded to dicker as follows.

Says Hank to Jim: 'I'll give you six pigs for a hoss; then you'll have twice as many critters in your drove as I will have in mine.'

Says Duke to Hank: 'I'll give you fourteen sheep for a hoss; then you'll have three times as many critters as I.'

Says Jim to Duke: 'I'll give you four cows for a hoss; then you'll have six times as many critters as I.'

How many animals all together?

A. 35
B. 36
C. 37
D. 38
E. 39

INDUSTRIAL

Test
4

ANSWERS

1.	B	11.	A
2.	C	12.	C
3.	B	13.	B
4.	A	14.	D
5.	C	15.	B
6.	D	16.	E
7.	D	17.	D
8.	B	18.	A
9.	A	19.	C
10.	B	20.	E

8-10	Average	14-16	Very good
11-13	Good	17-20	Exceptional

Verbal Section

This section tests your all-round ability in a wide range of verbal exercises including classification, antonyms, synonyms, and alternative meanings. They test your ability to innovate, adapt to different types of exercises quickly and work with speed to a set time limit.

There are four complete, separate tests numbered 1, 2, 3 and 4. Each test has ten parts numbered with Roman numerals. You should read through the instructions to each test carefully before commencing and then keep strictly to the time limit specified as any delay could invalidate your score. Calculators must not be used in the numerical tests (Part IX of Tests 1 and 2) but you may work out on paper any calculations which you think are necessary.

Do not spend too much time on any one question; if in doubt leave it and return to it in the time remaining. If you do not know an answer, have an intuitive guess, this may well be the correct answer.

Answers are given at the end of each test, but do not look at these until you have finished the whole test, in case you inadvertently read the solution to the next puzzle.

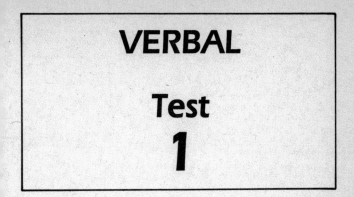

VERBAL

Test
1

VERBAL TEST 1

PART I

Synonyms (A)

Synonyms are words which mean the same or nearly the same as each other. You must find a word from the five choices given which you think means the same as the key word and underline that word.

Example	*Key word:* UNCTUOUS
Choose from:	swampy, frothy, oily, doughy, dizzy
Answer:	oily

You have six minutes in which to answer the ten questions.

Key word	Choose from
1. CHARMING	agreeable, delightful, ideal, elegant, virtuous
2. MEADOW	area, ground, space, lea, grass
3. DELETE	amend, adjust, erase, strike, cross
4. HEARSAY	gossip, talk, perception, review, eavesdrop
5. STRIDENT	gait, austere, precise, harsh, rivalry
6. SAVOUR	devour, flavour, prepare, cook, preserver
7. LARCENIST	criminal, receiver, thief, villain, informer
8. DIMPLE	chin, spot, cheek, depression, pimple
9. INCLEMENT	severe, discourteous, devious, merciful, gradient
10. PILGRIMAGE	visitation, odyssey, capsule, discovery, cognition

VERBAL TEST 1

PART I

Synonyms (A) — ANSWERS

1. delightful
2. lea
3. erase
4. gossip
5. harsh
6. flavour
7. thief
8. depression
9. severe
10. odyssey

4-5	**Average**	**8-9**	**Very good**
6-7	**Good**	**10**	**Exceptional**

VERBAL TEST 1

PART II

Synonyms (B)

Synonyms are words which mean the same or nearly the same as each other. From the six words given, find the two which mean the same as each other and underline those two words.

Example

Choose from: honeycomb, niche, grotto, recess, warren, trough

Answer: niche, recess

You have eight minutes in which to answer the ten questions.

Choose from

1. coarse, loud, blunt, rough, hard, angry
2. amend, influence, justify, deserve, find, excuse
3. unrivalled, shallow, strange, supercilious, heroic, haughty
4. learn, pupil, master, seek, college, book
5. admit, salute, preside, respect, welcome, enter
6. motivate, insult, calculate, estimate, list, answer
7. flattery, falsify, sarcasm, vanity, insipidity, cajolery
8. book, motto, speech, sign, maxim, memorandum
9. tawdry, stale, old, cheap, plentiful, poor
10. smooth, hollow, flat, solid, round, concave

VERBAL TEST 1

PART II

Synonyms (A) — ANSWERS

1. coarse, rough
2. justify, excuse
3. supercilious, haughty
4. learn, master
5. salute, welcome
6. calculate, estimate
7. flattery, cajolery
8. motto, maxim
9. tawdry, cheap
10. hollow, concave

4-5	**Average**	**8-9**	**Very good**
6-7	**Good**	**17-20**	**Exceptional**

VERBAL TEST 1

PART III

Antonyms (A)

Antonyms are words which mean the opposite or nearly the opposite to each other. You must find a word from the five choices given which you think means the opposite to the key word, and underline that word.

Example	*Key word:* CORPULENCE
Choose from:	grandiosity, slimness, obesity, vastness, bulkiness
Answer:	slimness

You have six minutes in which to answer the ten questions.

Key word	**Choose from**
1. TACIT	still, spoken, aware, rash, irregular
2. PACIFY	change, calm, allow, incite, allay
3. SHIELD	preserve, expose, strip, protect, proceed
4. UNIQUE	peculiar, straight, usual, different, expensive
5. IRRESOLUTE	pitiful, steadfast, sly, unsteady, regular
6. DULL	ordinary, fine, clear, far, vivid
7. PALPABLE	manifest, regular, obscure, difficult, worthless
8. ILLICIT	wrong, good, fair, legal, base
9. SAFE	precarious, slippy, loose, sound, free
10. FRESH	raw, late, asleep, weary, rest

VERBAL TEST 1

PART III

Antonyms (A) — ANSWERS

1. spoken
2. incite
3. expose
4. usual
5. steadfast
6. vivid
7. obscure
8. legal
9. precarious
10. weary

4-5	Average	8-9	Very good
6-7	Good	10	Exceptional

VERBAL TEST 1

PART IV

Antonyms (B)

Antonyms are words which mean the opposite or nearly the opposite to each other. From the six words given, find two which mean the opposite to each other and underline those two words.

Example

Choose from:	intriguing, resentful, impetuous, cautious, overpowering, exhilarating
Answer:	impetuous, cautious

Choose from

1. precise, approximate, near, careless, indistinct, partial
2. unwell, fresh, sombre, unhappy, poor, bright
3. senseless, empty, dull, busy, occupied, withdrawn
4. pollute, boil, purify, wash, clean, dissolve
5. tenderness, apathy, sadness, action, wisdom, concern
6. calm, worried, tempestuous, egotistical, fresh, helpful
7. friendly, anxious, timid, careless, intrepid, excited
8. stop, breed, prevent, inject, absolve, exterminate
9. fruitful, prolix, wasteful, charming, concise, silent
10. regular, listed, unknown, narrow, slow, variable

VERBAL TEST 1

PART IV

Antonyms (B) — ANSWERS

1. precise, careless
2. sombre, bright
3. empty, occupied
4. pollute, purify
5. apathy, concern
6. calm, tempestuous
7. timid, intrepid
8. breed, exterminate
9. prolix, concise
10. regular, variable

4-5	Average	8-9	Very good
6-7	Good	10	Exceptional

VERBAL TEST 1

PART V

Comparisons

Comparisons are a classification where an object or an idea is compared to another object or idea. You have to find the same connection with another word or idea. You have five possible answers from which to choose. Underline your choice of word.

Example   COURT is to TENNIS
                    as PISTE is to: cricket, hockey, skiing,
                                  golf, polo

Answer: skiing

You have eight minutes in which to answer the ten questions.

1. WHERE is to SHEFFIELD as WHEN is to:
   train, soon, how, maybe, time
2. LATHE is to WOOD as LOOM is to:
   material, textile, yarn, machine, apparatus
3. SANDBOY is to HAPPY as JUDGE is to:
   sad, justice, sober, serious, wig
4. GRACE is to ARCHBISHOP as EXCELLENCY is to:
   ambassador, prince, baron, archdeacon, duke
5. FOREWORD is to BOOK as OVERTURE is to:
   music, play, orchestra, composer, opera
6. PARE is to PEEL as FRAY is to:
   cut, rub, sever, incise, dissect
7. CLOSED is to SHUT as OPEN is to:
   overt, concluded, obscure, obfuscated, window
8. SPINACH is to VEGETABLE as SPHAGNUM is to:
   grass, soil, fruit, onion, moss
9. NORTH is to DIRECTION as RED is to:
   embarrassed, colour, ripe, orange, shade
10. MAHOGANY is to WOOD as GORSE is to:
    tree, shrub, plant, flower, spine

VERBAL TEST 1

PART V

Comparisons — ANSWERS

1. soon
2. yarn
3. sober
4. ambassador
5. opera
6. rub
7. overt
8. moss
9. colour
10. shrub

| 4-5 | Average | 8-9 | Very good |
| 6-7 | Good | 10 | Exceptional |

VERBAL TEST 1

PART VI

Links

Links are where two words are given which can be linked by a third word. You have to find a linking word which, placed on the end of the first word and placed in front of the second word, produces another word. Each dot represents a letter.

Example   play . . . nib

Answer: pen

You have eight minutes in which to answer the ten questions.

1. leg   . . .   lier
2. ball   . . . . . less
3. high   . . . .   lord
4. salt   . . . . . fall
5. dog   . . .   end
6. top   . . . .   on
7. south   . . . .   robe
8. life   . . . .   age
9. ran   . . . .   cloth
10. up   . . .   less

VERBAL TEST 1

PART VI

Links — Answers

1. ate
2. point
3. land
4. water
5. leg
6. less
7. ward
8. line
9. sack
10. end

4-5	**Average**	8-9	**Very good**
6-7	**Good**	10	**Exceptional**

VERBAL TEST 1

PART VII

Double Meaning

Double meaning is a system where a word has two meanings. You are given the two meanings and you have to find the word which applies to both meanings. Each dot represents a letter.

Example   Soldier's dormitory .... shouts and jeers

Answer: barracks

You have eight minutes in which to answer the ten questions.

1. eating place for
   service personnel   . . . .   state of confusion
2. narrow beam of light   . . .   type of fish
3. uppermost part   . . .   a toy
4. mock movement as   narrowest rule in
   in boxing   . . . . .   ruled paper
5. plan of action   . . . . . . insurance document
6. dark viscid substance . . .   informal word for
                                       seaman
7. cargo store   . . . .   keep in the hand
8. hybrid animal   . . . .   backless shoe
9. payment for   a slit or opening
   occupation   . . . .   made by tearing
10. leather glove   . . . . a punishing run

VERBAL TEST 1

PART VII

Double Meaning — ANSWERS

1. mess
2. ray
3. top
4. feint
5. policy
6. tar
7. hold
8. mule
9. rent
10. gauntlet

4-5	Average	8-9	Very good
6-7	Good	10	Exceptional

VERBAL TEST 1

PART VIII

ANAGRAMS

Anagrams are words which, when the letters are rearranged, spell out another word. Find a word from the following ten selections.

Example   more tiny   *Answer*:   enormity

You have twenty minutes in which to solve the ten puzzles.

1.   paul rice
2.   clap nine
3.   curb hero
4.   fine mast
5.   dear gene
6.   petes lad
7.   scare not
8.   poor fund
9.   near vote
10. pear teas

VERBAL TEST 1

PART VIII

Anagrams — ANSWERS

1. peculiar
2. pinnacle
3. brochure
4. manifest
5. renegade
6. pedestal
7. ancestor
8. profound
9. renovate
10. separate

4-5	Average	8-9	Very good
6-7	Good	10	Exceptional

VERBAL TEST 1

PART IX

Number Sequences

A sequence of numbers is given and you have to work out the number which will continue the sequence that is occurring.

Example   2, 4, 6, 8, 10, ?   *Answer*:   12

You have twelve minutes in which to answer the ten questions.

1. 1, 1.5, 2.5, 4, ?
2. 25, 23, 20, 16, ?
3. 5, 10, 10, 8, 15, 6, ?
4. 0, 1, 3, 4, 6, ?
5. 2, 5, 10, 17, 26, ?
6. 0, 3, 3, 6, 9, 15, ?
7. 1, 8, 27, 64, ?
8. 1, 1, 2, 6, 24, ?
9. 0.5, 0.55, 0.65, 0.8, ?
10. 1, 0.5, 0.333, 0.25, 0.2, ?

VERBAL TEST 1

PART IX

Number Sequences — ANSWERS

1. 6
2. 11
3. 20
4. 7
5. 37
6. 24
7. 125
8. 120
9. 1
10. 0.1666

4-5	Average	8-9	Very good
6-7	Good	10	Exceptional

VERBAL TEST 1

PART X

Classification

Classification is where a group of objects or ideas include one word which does not belong to that group. You have to select that word from each of the groups.

Example   pine, fir, elm, spruce, hemlock

Answer: ELM is a hardwood, the remainder are softwoods.

You have six minutes in which to select your ten words.

1. furore, commotion, noise, uproar, disturbance
2. dowager, duke, marchioness, baroness, princess
3. mantle, cloak, shawl, blouse, wrap
4. absolute, categorical, certain, possible, explicit
5. laugh, joke, smirk, giggle, titter
6. stall, chamber, cell, theatre, cubicle
7. soar, orbit, rise, ascend, climb
8. abrupt, soon, hasty, sudden, impulsive
9. drill, polish, file, rasp, smooth
10. timorous, startled, coy, retiring, irresolute

VERBAL TEST 1

PART X

Classification — ANSWERS

1. noise
2. duke
3. blouse
4. possible
5. joke
6. theatre
7. orbit
8. soon
9. drill
10. startled

4-5	**Average**	**8-9**	**Very good**
6-7	**Good**	**10**	**Exceptional**

TOTAL SCORE VERBAL TEST 1

40-59	**Average**	**80-90**	**Very good**
60-79	**Good**	**91-100**	**Exceptional**

VERBAL

Test
2

VERBAL TEST 2

PART I

Synonyms (A)

Synonyms are words which mean the same or nearly the same as each other. You must find a word from the five choices given which you think means the same as the key word and underline that word.

Example	*Key word:* UNCTUOUS
Choose from:	swampy, frothy, oily, doughy, dizzy
Answer:	oily

You have six minutes in which to answer the ten questions.

Key word	**Choose from**
1. OBSESS	idea, think, engross, engage, witness
2. VILIFY	shout, malign, reply, argue, insist
3. AFICIONADO	official, steward, organiser, devotee, lawyer
4. SUCCINCT	concise, fresh, marked, sudden, orderly
5. DIAMETRIC	geometric, contrary, angled, lined, circular
6. SWIRL	oscillate, veer, vibrate, spin, swing
7. STAMINA	success, indefatigability, health, will-power, daring
8. COUPON	bill, cheque, slip, goods, list
9. WAX	substance, enlarge, candle, heat, weaken
10. COALESCE	mine, shift, burn, seek, fuse

VERBAL TEST 2

PART I

Synonyms (A) — ANSWERS

1. engross
2. malign
3. devotee
4. concise
5. contrary
6. spin
7. indefatigability
8. slip
9. enlarge
10. fuse

4-5	Average	8-9	Very good
6-7	Good	10	Exceptional

VERBAL TEST 2

PART II

Synonyms (B)

Synonyms are words which mean the same or nearly the same as each other. From the six words given, find the two which mean the same as each other and underline those two words.

Example:

Choose from: honeycomb, niche, grotto, recess, warren, trough

Answer: niche, recess

You have eight minutes in which to answer the ten questions.

Choose from

1. holiday, retirement, time, abroad, vacation, summer
2. pied, dark, piper, grey, coloured, dappled
3. place, stance, stem, height, posture, type
4. concentrate, change, dilute, weaken, finish, heat
5. yield, vouch, elect, charge, check, certify
6. point, eye, brow, slope, nadir, peak
7. concept, practise, pride, hypothesis, camouflage, ideal
8. aspire, secede, finalise, arrive, isolate, withdraw
9. build, dodge, contrive, estimate, fabricate, regret
10. trigger, pull, gun, aim, race, start

VERBAL TEST 2

PART II

Synonyms (B) — ANSWERS

1. holiday, vacation
2. pied, dappled
3. stance, posture
4. dilute, weaken
5. vouch, certify
6. brow, peak
7. concept, hypothesis
8. secede, withdraw
9. contrive, fabricate
10. trigger, start

| 4-5 | Average | 8-9 | Very good |
| 6-7 | Good | 10 | Exceptional |

VERBAL TEST 2

PART III

Antonyms (A)

Antonyms are words which mean the opposite or nearly the opposite to each other. You must find a word from the five choices given which you think means the opposite to the key word, and underline that word.

Example:　　　*Key word:* CORPULENCE

Choose from:　　grandiosity, slimness, obesity, vastness, bulkiness

Answer:　　　slimness

You have six minutes in which to answer the ten questions.

Key word	**Choose from**
1. PRIDE	disenchantment, disappointment, anger, greed, humility
2. LATER	never, previous, soon, now, when
3. UNION	confederation, rupture, divorce, alteration, junction
4. CUNNING	artless, wily, selfish, dishonesty, unwise
5. PREFACE	text, postscript, result, solution, amend
6. IMPARTIALITY	equity, completeness, friendship, subjectiveness, prejudice
7. REASONABLE	cruel, preposterous, bad, strange, unwell
8. DISCORD	harmony, incongruity, fairness, joy, elation
9. RASH	foolish, slow, calm, normal, guarded
10. PRAISE	hope, defamation, characterise, ignore, worry

VERBAL TEST 2

PART III

Antonyms (A) — ANSWERS

1. humility
2. previous
3. rupture
4. artless
5. postscript
6. prejudice
7. preposterous
8. harmony
9. guarded
10. defamation

4-5	Average	8-9	Very good
6-7	Good	10	Exceptional

VERBAL TEST 2

PART IV

Antonyms (B)

Antonyms are words which mean the opposite or nearly
the opposite to each other. From the six words given,
find two which mean the opposite to each other and
underline those two words.

Example

Choose from: intriguing, resentful, impetuous,
cautious, overpowering, exhilarating

Answer: impetuous, cautious

You have eight minutes in which to answer the ten
questions.

Choose from

1. construct, support, free, despise, abandon, check
2. grave, worried, angry, facetious, pleasant, fluent
3. wealth, glory, loneliness, wisdom, sorrow,
    obscurity
4. induced, clear, permanent, ephemeral, deep,
    religious
5. deadly, breathtaking, serious, calm, officious,
    beneficial
6. terrorise, extenuate, argue, victimise, cheer,
    aggravate
7. spurious, scornful, sudden, authentic,
    manufactured, courageous
8. influence, appease, worry, bribe, enrage, deject
9. hard, pungent, happy, flavoured, oily, mild
10. provoke, clarify, pretend, unite, assuage, astute

VERBAL TEST 2

PART IV

Antonyms (B) — ANSWERS

1. support, abandon
2. grave, facetious
3. glory, obscurity
4. permanent, ephemeral
5. deadly, beneficial
6. extenuate, aggravate
7. spurious, authentic
8. appease, enrage
9. pungent, mild
10. provoke, assuage

4-5	Average	8-9	Very good
6-7	Good	10	Exceptional

VERBAL TEST 2

PART V

Comparisons

Comparisons are a classification where an object or an idea is compared to another object or idea. You have to find the same connection with another word or idea. You have five possible answers from which to choose. Underline your choice of word.

Example   COURT is to TENNIS
                as PISTE is to:
                cricket, hockey, skiing, golf, polo

Answer: skiing

You have eight minutes in which to answer the ten questions.

1. SPEED is to MOVEMENT as MUSIC is to:
    musician, notes, instrument, song, sound
2. SCHILLING is to AUSTRIA as POUND is to:
    Australia, Iceland, Fiji, Malta, New Zealand
3. OPTIMISM is to HOPE as PESSIMISM is to:
    despair, expectation, evil, fear, news
4. CONVECTION is to HEAT as ILLUMINATION is to:
    wavelength, light, magnification, spectrum, sight
5. KILOGRAM is to WEIGHT as PINT is to:
    liquid, volume, capacity, metric, gallon
6. MEAN is to GENEROUS as AGITATION is to:
    water, temper, calmness, levity, emotion
7. ISLET is to ISLAND as Hill is to:
    slope, elevation, mountain, knoll, tor
8. RANCID is to TASTE as MALODOROUS is to:
    melody, sound, smell, touch, feelings
9. BOVINE is to CATTLE as PISCINE is to:
    sheep, fish, seaweed, pigs, frogs
10. D.D.T. is to ABBREVIATION as LASER is to:
    antithesis, epigram, word, acronym, imagery

VERBAL TEST 2

PART V

Comparisons — ANSWERS

1. sound
2. Malta
3. despair
4. light
5. capacity
6. calmness
7. mountain
8. smell
9. fish
10. acronym

4-5	**Average**	**8-9**	**Very good**
6-7	**Good**	**10**	**Exceptional**

VERBAL TEST 2

PART VI

Links

Links are where two words are given which can be linked by a third word. You have to find a linking word which, placed on the end of the first word and placed in front of the second word, produces another word. Each dot represents a letter.

Example   play   . . .   nib

Answer: pen

You have eight minutes in which to answer the ten questions.

1. note   . . . . .   clip
2. show   . . . .   fall
3. drag   . . .   ball
4. tan   . .   at
5. mid   . . . .   end
6. spot   . . . . .   weight
7. pass   . . .   less
8. snow   . . .   age
9. one   . . . .   less
10. play   . . . . . . work

VERBAL TEST 2

PART VI

Links – ANSWERS

1. paper
2. down
3. net
4. go
5. week
6. light
7. age
8. man
9. self
10. ground

4-5	**Average**	8-9	**Very good**
6-7	**Good**	10	**Exceptional**

VERBAL TEST 2

PART VII

Double Meaning

Double meaning is a system where a word has two
meanings. You are given the two meanings and you have
to find the word which applies to both meanings. Each
dot represents a letter.

Example   Soldier's dormitory . . . . shouts and jeers

Answer: barracks

You have eight minutes in which to answer the ten
questions.

1. hang back	. . .	cover cylinder
2. slap smartly	. . . . .	sailing vessel
3. an intentionally misleading explanation	. . . . .	lustre or sheen
4. the back or hind part	. . . .	to breed animals
5. a game	. . . .	an insect
6. something belonging to me	. . . .	system of excavations
7. profoundly wise man	. . . .	plant whose leaves are used in cooking
8. small open pie	. . . .	cutting, sharp
9. the barb of a harpoon	. . . . .	an accidental stroke of luck
10. to hurl or throw	. . . . .	heavy dark substance

VERBAL TEST 2

PART VII

Double Meaning — ANSWERS

1. lag
2. smack
3. gloss
4. rear
5. cricket
6. mine
7. sage
8. tart
9. fluke
10. pitch

| 4-5 | Average | 8-9 | Very good |
| 6-7 | Good | 10 | Exceptional |

VERBAL TEST 2

PART VIII

Anagrams

Anagrams are words which, when the letters are rearranged, spell out another word. Find a word from the following ten selections.

Example   more tiny   *Answer*:   enormity

You have twenty minutes in which to solve the ten puzzles.

1.   dose rats
2.   made coin
3.   cite acts
4.   save hide
5.   tore gash
6.   peas paul
7.   cure sore
8.   rome site
9.   tart face
10. torn name

VERBAL TEST 2

PART VIII

Anagrams — ANSWERS

1. assorted
2. comedian
3. ecstatic
4. adhesive
5. shortage
6. applause
7. resource
8. tiresome
9. artefact
10. ornament

| 4-5 | Average | 8-9 | Very good |
| 6-7 | Good | 10 | Exceptional |

VERBAL TEST 2

PART IX

Number Sequences

A sequence of numbers is given and you have to work out the number which will continue the sequence that is occurring.

Example   2, 4, 6, 8, 10 ?

Answer: 12

You have twelve minutes in which to answer the ten questions.

1.   1, 0.95, 0.85, 0.65, ?
2.   2, 5, 12, 27, 58, ?
3.   16, 16, 15, 17, 13, 19, 10, ?
4.   3, 2, 9, 4, 81, ?
5.   0.5, 2, 1, 6, 2, 18, ?
6.   48, 24, 16, 12, 9.6, ?
7.   1, 8, 22, 43, 71, ?
8.   0, 10, 10, 20, 30, 50, ?
9.   98, 88, 79, 71, ?
10. 45, 15, 41, 19, 38, 22, ?

VERBAL TEST 2

PART IX

Number Sequences — ANSWERS

1. 0.25
2. 121
3. 22
4. 16
5. 4
6. 8
7. 106
8. 80
9. 64
10. 36

| 4-5 | Average | 8-9 | Very good |
| 6-7 | Good | 10 | Exceptional |

VERBAL TEST 2

PART X

Classification

Classification is where a group of objects or ideas include one word which does not belong to that group. You have to select that word from each of the groups.

Example   pine, fir, elm, spruce, hemlock

Answer: ELM is a hardwood, the remainder are softwoods

You have six minutes in which to select your ten words.

1. hike, run, march, tramp, trudge
2. overturn, upset, invert, capsize, collapse
3. narrate, compose, recite, relate, declaim
4. intimidate, scare, terrorize, petrify, attack
5. angry, rash, volatile, fiery, impetuous
6. malefactor, victim, felon, transgressor, delinquent
7. oblique, sheer, inclined, tilted, sloped
8. fine, admirable, fair, choice, grand
9. dispatch, parcel, mail, post, forward
10. abstemiousness, sobriety, moderation, abstinence, indulgence

VERBAL TEST 2

PART X

Classification — ANSWERS

1. run
2. collapse
3. compose
4. attack
5. angry
6. victim
7. sheer
8. fair
9. parcel
10. indulgence

4-5	**Average**	**8-9**	**Very good**
6-7	**Good**	**10**	**Exceptional**

TOTAL SCORE VERBAL TEST 2

40-59	**Average**	80-90	**Very good**
60-79	**Good**	91-100	**Exceptional**

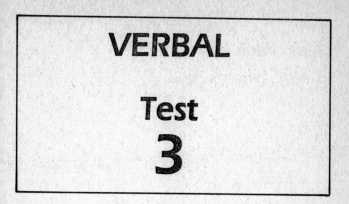

VERBAL

Test
3

VERBAL TEST 3

PART I

Synonyms (A)

Synonyms are words which mean the same or nearly the same as each other. You must find a word from the five choices given which you think means the same as the key word and underline that word.

Example	*Key word:* UNCTUOUS
Choose from:	swampy, frothy, oily, doughy, dizzy
Answer:	oily

You have six minutes in which to answer the ten questions.

Key word	**Choose from**
1. OBSCURE	slanting, abstruse, broken, certain, dejected
2. ACRID	reasonable, cooked, scorched, sour, sleepy
3. BESPEAK	gag, slice, open, listen, engage
4. CABAL	gang, alley, play, throw, space
5. STICK	polish, level, cleave, master, aid
6. LAW	statute, missile, strength, follow, artful
7. URBANE	foolish, growing, certain, suave, clever
8. EBRIETY	petty, aristocratic, form, freshness, dismal
9. HAGGARD	black, withered, wild, bloated, fearful
10. VALID	servant, pale, poor, open, defensible

VERBAL TEST 3

PART I

Synonyms (A) — ANSWERS

1. abstruse
2. sour
3. engage
4. gang
5. cleave
6. statute
7. suave
8. freshness
9. wild
10. defensible

4-5	Average	8-9	Very good
6-7	Good	10	Exceptional

VERBAL TEST 3

PART II

Synonyms (B)

Synonyms are words which mean the same or nearly the same as each other. From the six words given, find the two which mean the same as each other and underline those two words.

Example

Choose from: honeycomb, niche, grotto, recess, warren, trough

Answer: niche, recess

You have eight minutes in which to answer the ten questions.

Choose from

1. vernal, colourful, covered, Spring, present, lower
2. thick, fish, angry, turbid, awkward, cool
3. icon, zenith, summit, foreign, lisp, waspish
4. labour, camp, linger, wander, cool, travail
5. suggest, master, temper, strike, custom, wont
6. silence, sneeze, herald, mask, report, usher
7. vocal, write, record, verbal, scurry, fear
8. costume, birdlike, redress, right, miniature, habit
9. kind, family, ignite, shade, kindle, shadow
10. jubilee, regal, feast, royal, throne, jewel

VERBAL TEST 3

PART II

Synonyms (B) — ANSWERS

1. vernal, Spring
2. turbid, thick
3. zenith, summit
4. travail, labour
5. wont, custom
6. usher, herald
7. verbal, vocal
8. redress, right
9. kindle, ignite
10. regal, royal

| 4-5 | Average | 8-9 | Very good |
| 6-7 | Good | 10 | Exceptional |

VERBAL TEST 3

PART III

Antonyms (A)

Antonyms are words which mean the opposite or nearly the opposite to each other. You must find a word from the five choices given which you think means the opposite to the key word, and underline that word.

Example	*Key word:* CORPULENCE
Choose from:	grandiosity, slimness, obesity, vastness, bulkiness
Answer:	slimness

You have six minutes in which to answer the ten questions.

Key word	**Choose from**
1. DEVIOUS	straight, tension, bass, revision, overcast
2. FIDELITY	treachery, lightly, famously, musically, mobility
3. OBTUSE	altered, acute, radical, condition, unstable
4. DESTROY	build, advertise, puff, plague, fierce
5. DASHING	holding, brooding, testing, balancing, shrinking
6. CRABBED	caught, deserted, cordial, grounded, medicated
7. RAPACIOUS	frugal, precious, practised, calm, qualified
8. STOICAL	herbal, excitable, variable, methodical, magical
9. CONVULSE	train, precise, convention, compose, pulsate
10. YOKE	divorce, ovoid, administer, chemistry, bore

VERBAL TEST 3

PART III

Antonyms (A) – ANSWERS

1. straight
2. treachery
3. acute
4. build
5. shrinking
6. cordial
7. frugal
8. excitable
9. compose
10. divorce

| 4-5 | Average | 8-9 | Very good |
| 6-7 | Good | 10 | Exceptional |

VERBAL TEST 3

PART IV

Antonyms (B)

Antonyms are words which mean the opposite or nearly the opposite to each other. From the six words given, find two which mean the opposite to each other and underline those two words.

Example

Choose from: intriguing, resentful, impetuous, cautious, overpowering, exhilarating

Answer: impetuous, cautious

You have eight minutes in which to answer the ten questions.

Choose from

1. strip, fall, snub, slight, relate, drape
2. blame, default, famous, desert, action, hold
3. remind, argue, certain, equivocal, delicate, sentimental
4. motive, defence, leisure, grudge, perdition, eternity
5. familiar, ridiculous, ludicrous, decorative, praiseworthy, enjoyable
6. nugatory, sweetness, intern, treasure, important, globular
7. irrigate, satisfy, promulgate, special, massage, suppress
8. balance, disbelief, grandeur, tenet, stubborn, hurried
9. domestic, perfume, miser, vagrant, motherly, officer
10. compose, harbour, winnow, document, loser, strain

VERBAL TEST 3

PART IV

Antonyms (B) — ANSWERS

1. strip, drape
2. default, action
3. equivocal, certain
4. perdition, eternity
5. praiseworthy, ludicrous
6. nugatory, important
7. promulgate, suppress
8. disbelief, tenet
9. domestic, vagrant
10. compose, winnow

4-5	Average	8-9	Very good
6-7	Good	10	Exceptional

VERBAL TEST 3

PART V

Comparisons

Comparisons are a classification where an object or an idea is compared to another object or idea. You have to find the same connection with another word or idea. You have five possible answers from which to choose. Underline your choice of word.

Example   COURT is to TENNIS
                 as PISTE is to: cricket, hockey, skiing,
                                 golf, polo

Answer: skiing

You have eight minutes in which to answer the ten questions.

1. WEAK is to STRONG as HOT is to:
   tropic, water, tepid, cold, burn
2. BOOK is to LIBRARY as TREASURE is to:
   trove, museum, island, trail, pirate
3. PANDA is to BAMBOO is SILKWORM is to:
   mulberry, oak, aspen, willow, cedar
4. SPHERE is to BALL as TORUS is to:
   wedding, doughnut, boxing, fairy, toreador
5. HAND is to MAGICIAN as BATON is to:
   conductor, dancer, striker, hypnotist, sailor
6. WILDEBEEST is to GNU as CAMELOPARD is to:
   camel, leopard, giraffe, zebra, dromedary
7. SAUSAGE is to MASH as TRIPE is to:
   carrots, beans, chips, onions, cabbage
8. STRING is to VIOLIN as REED is to:
   pond, book, film, clarinet, guitar
9. SWEATER is to WOOL as SHAGREEN is to:
   corduroy, silk, leather, cotton, tulle
10. TIBIA is to LEG as METACARPUS is to:
    arm, head, foot, ankle, shoulder

VERBAL TEST 3

PART V

Comparisons — ANSWERS

1. cold
2. museum
3. mulberry
4. doughnut
5. conductor
6. giraffe
7. onions
8. clarinet
9. leather
10. hand

4-5	Average	8-9	Very good
6-7	Good	10	Exceptional

VERBAL TEST 3

PART VI

Links

Links are where two words are given which can be linked by a third word. You have to find a linking word which, placed on the end of the first word and placed in front of the second word, produces another word. Each dot represents a letter.

Example   play . . . nib

Answer: pen

You have eight minutes in which to answer the ten questions.

1. butter   . . .   trap
2. book   . . . .   hole
3. bird   . . . .   time
4. film   . . . .   dust
5. spider   . . . . .   pot
6. shell   . . . .   paste
7. book   . . . .   time
8. kidney   . . . .   sprout
9. paper   . . .   friend
10. buck   . . .   part

VERBAL TEST 3

PART VI

Links — Answers

1. fly
2. worm
3. bath
4. star
5. plant
6. fish
7. mark
8. bean
9. boy
10. ram

4-5	Average	8-9	Very good
6-7	Good	10	Exceptional

VERBAL TEST 3

PART VII

Double Meaning

Double meaning is a system where a word has two meanings. You are given the two meanings and you have to find the word which applies to both meanings. Each dot represents a letter.

Example   Soldier's dormitory .... shouts and jeers

Answer: barracks

You have eight minutes in which to answer the ten questions.

1. book   .... store for arms
2. oriental   .... googly by
                                       left-handed bowler
3. halo   ...... cloud
4. percussion instrument. ...... geometrical figure
5. motor cycle
   attachment   ...... cocktail
6. aquatic rear part   .... dance step
7. sundial rod   .... part of a square that
                                       is left when a smaller
                                       square is removed
8. small dagger   ....
                                       hinged seat in
                                       church
9. type of turtle   ...... type of fish
10. trousers   .... type of buoy

VERBAL TEST 3

PART VII

Double Meaning — ANSWERS

1. magazine
2. chinaman
3. nimbus
4. triangle
5. sidecar
6. fishtail
7. gnomon
8. misericord
9. snapper
10. breeches

4-5	Average	8-9	Very good
6-7	Good	10	Exceptional

VERBAL TEST 3

PART VIII

ANAGRAMS

Anagrams are words which, when the letters are rearranged, spell out another word. Find a word from the following ten selections.

Example   more tiny   *Answer*:   enormity

You have twenty minutes in which to solve the ten puzzles.

1. bias bull
2. shot pill
3. neat film
4. neat glib
5. mood tans
6. flat romp
7. stem rang
8. rave mick
9. stop sing
10. teen date

VERBAL TEST 3

PART VIII

Anagrams -- ANSWERS

1. sillabub
2. hilltops
3. filament
4. tangible
5. mastodon
6. platform
7. garments
8. maverick
9. signpost
10. edentate

4-5	**Average**	8-9	**Very good**
6-7	**Good**	10	**Exceptional**

VERBAL TEST 3

PART IX

Sequence

A sequence is given and from the choice of five alternatives you have to select the one which you think will continue the sequence to a definite rule or reason.

Example   LT FA E

Choose from: N, W, H , I, K

Answer: W

You have twelve minutes in which to answer the ten questions.

1. breeze, wind, mistral, sirocco, chinook, ?
   Choose from: earthquake, thunder, hurricane, tornado, waterspout
2. C, O, S, U, P, ?
   Choose from: L, Z, T, R, X
3. prism, cube, cone, sphere, cylinder, ?
   Choose from: dodecahedron, trapezoid, circle, triangle, nonagon
4. foggy, hazy, misty, murky, smoky, ?
   Choose from: lucid, limp, turbid, turgid, diaphanous
5. coupé, sedan, saloon, limousine, roadster, ?
   Choose from: caravel, flivver, carrack, gallivat, ferry
6. brook, creek, burn, bourse, runnel, ?
   Choose from: pampas, tundra, atoll, rill, archipelago
7. octagon, rectangle, square, oblong, pentagon, ?
   Choose from: trapezium, cuboid, sigma, nodal, logarithm
8. bark, yelp, yap, snap, growl, ?
   Choose from: cackle, whine, crow, tweet, cluck

9. picquet, cribbage, euchre, whist, canasta, ?
Choose from: nautch, curling, bezique, squash,
speleology
10. coven, rake, wide, hover, drift, ?
Choose from: craven, slide, rafter, birth, haven

VERBAL TEST 3

PART IX

Sequence — ANSWERS

1. hurricane
2. R
3. dodecahedron
4. turbid
5. flivver
6. rill
7. trapezium
8. whine
9. bezique
10. rafter

4-5	Average	8-9	Very good
6-7	Good	10	Exceptional

TOTAL SCORE VERBAL TEST 3

40-59	Average	80-90	Very good
60-79	Good	91-100	Exceptional

VERBAL TEST 3

PART X

Classification

Classification is where a group of objects or ideas include one word which does not belong to that group. You have to select that word from each of the groups.

Example   pine, fir, elm, spruce, hemlock

Answer: ELM is a hardwood, the remainder are softwoods.

You have six minutes in which to select your ten words.

1.   Luke, Mark, Oliver, Matthew, John
2.   prawn, lobster, shrimp, crab, cray
3.   Siamese, Burmese, Chinchilla, Abyssinian, Manx
4.   dorsal, pelvic, caudal, lateral, pectoral
5.   raven, rook, blackbird, jay, jackdaw
6.   Susanne, Hilary, Muriel, Shelagh, Lydia
7.   London, Washington, Manchester, Melbourne, Vienna
8.   raspberry, strawberry, redcurrant, blackcurrant, gooseberry
9.   doe, hob, sow, bitch, mare
10.   quart, gallon, peck, puncheon, hogshead

VERBAL TEST 3

PART X

Classification – ANSWERS

1. Oliver
2. crab
3. Chinchilla
4. lateral
5. blackbird
6. Hilary
7. Melbourne
8. strawberry
9. hob
10. peck

4-5	Average	8-9	Very good
6-7	Good	10	Exceptional

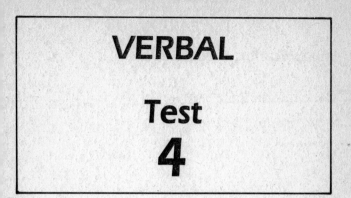

VERBAL

Test
4

VERBAL TEST 4

PART I

Synonyms (A)

Synonyms are words which mean the same or nearly the same as each other. You must find a word from the five choices given which you think means the same as the key word and underline that word.

Example	*Key word:* UNCTUOUS
Choose from:	swampy, frothy, oily, doughy, dizzy
Answer:	oily

You have six minutes in which to answer the ten questions.

Key word	Choose from
1. KEN	chop, keen, view, open, wrench
2. SHACKLE	shed, smash, rattle, husk, fetter
3. LATENT	spongy, secret, lost, shiny, falsehood
4. STIPULATE	handle, splatter, consume, topple, agree
5. FLIPPANT	gasping, webbed, loose, forward, harsh
6. BUD	germ, friend, hack, outcome, mate
7. HALCYON	large, warm, serene, horizon, lazy
8. FOIBLE	tale, fault, gargle, toy, habit
9. DEROGATE	opening, adopt, forsake, detract, residence
10. CORUSCATE	flash, twist, scrub, inflate, glide

VERBAL TEST 4

PART I

Synonyms (A) — ANSWERS

1. view
2. fetter
3. secret
4. agree
5. forward
6. germ
7. serene
8. fault
9. detract
10. flash

4-5	Average	8-9	Very good
6-7	Good	10	Exceptional

VERBAL TEST 4

PART II

Synonyms (B)

Synonyms are words which mean the same or nearly the same as each other. From the six words given, find the two which mean the same as each other and underline those two words.

Example

Choose from: honeycomb, niche, grotto, recess, warren, trough

Answer: niche, recess

You have eight minutes in which to answer the ten questions.

Choose from

1. auspicious, secretive, favourable, guilty, worldy, hidden
2. perfect, blissful, supine, yearn, lazy, edible
3. haunt, plaint, ascend, promote, taunt, upbraid
4. tyro, thread, teacher, wheel, novice, ghost
5. flake, wizened, ease, weazon, pest, smooth
6. attenuate, narrow, impress, maintain, listen, straighten
7. pitiful, sad, pithy, covering, beneath, terse
8. boil, bruise, soak, fester, imbrue, wrap
9. smothered, frugal, frozen, alpine, muted, sparing
10. prosaic, dull, pattern, champion, speaker, design

VERBAL TEST 4

PART II

Synonyms (B) — ANSWERS

1. auspicious, favourable
2. supine, lazy
3. upbraid, taunt
4. tyro, novice
5. weazon, wizened
6. attenuate, narrow
7. pithy, terse
8. imbrue, soak
9. frugal, sparing
10. prosaic, dull

4-5	Average	8-9	Very good
6-7	Good	10	Exceptional

VERBAL TEST 4

PART III

Antonyms (B)

Antonyms are words which mean the opposite or nearly
the opposite to each other. You must find a word from
the five choices given which you think means the
opposite to the key word, and underline that word.

Example	*Key word:* CORPULENCE
Choose from:	grandiosity, slimness, obesity, vastness, bulkiness
Answer:	slimness

You have six minutes in which to answer the ten
questions.

	Key word	Choose from
1.	GAMBOL	speak, wager, tire, chain, enquire
2.	REFLECT	promise, learn, prop, dream, depend
3.	SANCTIFY	harmonize, dispel, obliterate, prove, pollute
4.	FLOUNDER	flow, cad, bloom, sharp, stagger
5.	WHEEDLE	sweep, scare, moan, thrive, leer
6.	VAPID	damp, cloudy, animated, spring, opaque
7.	STAVE	note, press, cleanse, serve, court
8.	LICIT	straight, unfair, strike, mean, docile
9.	GUILE	candour, cover, loyalty, veil, thought
10.	EMOLLIENT	pale, follower, treasure, galling, patient

VERBAL TEST 4

PART III

Antonyms (B) — ANSWERS

1. tire
2. dream
3. pollute
4. flow
5. scare
6. animated
7. court
8. unfair
9. candour
10. galling

4-5	Average	8-9	Very good
6-7	Good	10	Exceptional

VERBAL TEST 4

PART IV

Antonyms (B)

Antonyms are words which mean the opposite or nearly
the opposite to each other. From the six words given,
find two which mean the opposite to each other and
underline those two words.

Example

Choose from: intriguing, resentful, impetuous,
                cautious, overpowering, exhilarating

Answer: impetuous, cautious

You have eight minutes in which to answer the ten
questions.

Choose from

1. cogitate, maunder, fallen, amble, agitate, bankrupt
2. acrid, calm, firm, flaccid, aggressive, roasted
3. informer, delude, hoyden, active, flourishing, prude
4. evening, motherly, sensitive, rebound, matutinal, waking
5. minimize, proffer, detain, prudent, shower, correct
6. salve, effort, defect, hurt, imprison, dagger
7. acknowledge, wild, absurd, urge, martyr, waive
8. clever, intrigue, hibernal, humid, balmy, slough
9. praise, ancillary, neutral, farewell, alien, superior
10. acquiesce, forgive, object, watery, muted, misery

PART IV

Antonyms (B) — ANSWERS

1   cogitate, maunder
2.   flaccid, firm
3.   hoyden, prude
4.   evening, matutinal
5.   proffer, detain
6.   salve, hurt
7.   urge, waive
8.   hibernal, balmy
9.   ancillary, alien
10.   acquiesce, object

4-5	Average	8-9	Very good
6-7	Good	10	Exceptional

VERBAL TEST 4

PART V

Comparisons

Comparisons are a classification where an object or an idea is compared to another object or idea. You have to find the same connection with another word or idea. You have five possible answers from which to choose. Underline your choice of word.

Example   COURT is to TENNIS
               as PISTE is to: cricket, hockey, skiing,
                                golf, polo

Answer: skiing

You have eight minutes in which to answer the ten questions.

1. MAN is to WOMAN as BOY is to:
   lad, child, girl, son, brother
2. ROSE is to BUSH as APPLE is to:
   pie, cook, tree, orchard, eat
3. NAIL is to FINGER as HAIR is to:
   comb, brush, mat, head, broom
4. SHEEP is to WOOL as GOAT is to:
   farm, mohair, grass, beard, field
5. SOLDIER is to BATTLE as PLAYER is to:
   team, partner, ground, school, game
6. HAMMER is to NAIL as NEEDLE is to:
   material, thread, sew, sharp, stitch
7. LIGHT is to DAY as DARK is to:
   blind, dim, black, night, sombre
8. MADRAS is to COTTON FABRIC as MADRIGAL is to:
   song, dance, illness, asylum, flower
9. GRATICULE is to FINE LINES as MELISMA is to:
   music, sweetness, speech, bliss, smell
10. ALIFORM is to WING-SHAPED as ENISFORM is to:
    barrel-shaped, pea-shaped, sword-shaped, wedge-shaped, cone-shaped

VERBAL TEST 4

PART V

Comparisons — ANSWERS

1. girl
2. tree
3. head
4. mohair
5. game
6. thread
7. night
8. song
9. music
10. sword-shaped

4-5	Average	8-9	Very good
6-7	Good	10	Exceptional

VERBAL TEST 4

PART VI

Links

Links are where two words are given which can be linked
by a third word. You have to find a linking word which,
placed on the end of the first word and placed in front of
the second word, produces another word. Each dot
represents a letter.

Example   play . . . nib

Answer: pen

You have eight minutes in which to answer the ten
questions.

1.	mouse	. . . .	door
2.	stage	. . . .	bag
3.	news	. . . . . .	rack
4.	clothes	. . . . .	race
5.	harvest	. . . .	table
6.	billiard	. . . . .	linen
7.	hose	. . . .	dream
8.	birthday	. . . .	cards
9.	chain	. . .	dust
10.	lucky	. . . .	bridge

Links — Answers

1. trap
2. hand
3. letter
4. horse
5. time
6. table
7. pipe
8. greeting
9. saw
10. draw

| 4-5 | **Average** | 8-9 | **Very good** |
| 6-7 | **Good** | 10 | **Exceptional** |

VERBAL TEST 4

PART VII

Double Meaning

Double meaning is a system where a word has two meanings. You are given the two meanings and you have to find the word which applies to both meanings. Each dot represents a letter.

Example   Soldier's dormitory .... shouts and jeers

Answer: barracks

You have eight minutes in which to answer the ten questions.

1. kiss hastily   . . . .   measure
2. loose blouse   . . . . biscuit
3. high moorland   . . . .   ruthless
4. ruled lines   . . . . .   sham attack
5. flat-bottomed skiff . . . .   fish
6. right-hand side of
    shield   . . . . . .   Irish cattle
7. knitted woollen jacket . . . . Welsh county
8. flag fabric   . . . . bird
9. stupid person   . . . . .   small gannet
10. glass for spirits   . . . . . . rest for a cue

Double Meaning — ANSWERS

1. peck
2. garibaldi
3. fell
4. feint
5. dory
6. dexter
7. Cardigan
8. bunting
9. booby
10. jigger

| 4-5 | Average | 8-9 | Very good |
| 6-7 | Good | 10 | Exceptional |

VERBAL TEST 4

PART VIII

ANAGRAMS

Anagrams are words which, when the letters are rearranged, spell out another word. Find a word from the following ten selections.

Example   more tiny   *Answer*:   enormity

You have twenty minutes in which to solve the ten puzzles.

1. cut perm
2. core plate
3. been marm
4. sing roar
5. send rail
6. lapel pant
7. near bump
8. slick past
9. or rutted
10. paste lout

VERBAL TEST 4

PART VIII

Anagrams — ANSWERS

1. crumpet
2. percolate
3. membrane
4. garrison
5. islander
6. appellant
7. penumbra
8. slapstick
9. tortured
10. postulate

| 4-5 | Average | | 8-9 | Very good |
| 6-7 | Good | | 10 | Exceptional |

VERBAL TEST 4

PART IX

Sequence

A sequence is given and from the choice of five alternatives you have to select the one which you think will continue the sequence to a definite rule or reason.

Example   LT   FA   E
Choose from: N, W, H, I, K
Answer: W

You have twelve minutes to answer the ten questions.

1. threshold, cill, lintel, fascia, tile, ?
    Choose from: door, window, chimney, porch, bell
2. sprat, carp, chub, trout, tunney, ?
    Choose from: whitebait, grouper, grilse, salmon, herring
3. shoe, sock, trousers, shirt, collar, ?
    Choose from: beret, stole, camisole, belt, sari
4. 8, 27, 64, 125, 216, ?
    Choose from: 303, 313, 323, 333, 343
5. a, as, sat, taps, traps, ?
    Choose from: sparse, sparta, sprain, trains, sprint
6. cranium, scapula, sternum, humerus, femur, ?
    Choose from: diaphragm, ureter, fibula, choroid, sclera
7. O, M, Q, K, S, ?
    Choose from: G, H, I, J, L
8. one, o , two, w, three, r, four, ?
    Choose from: t, u, o, f, r
9. helix, concha, lobule, malleus, incus, ?
    Choose from: pineal, thymus, stapes, ganglion, axon
10. asteroid, comet, planet, star, nebula, ?
    Choose from: black hole, nova, galaxy, quark, atom

VERBAL TEST 4

PART IX

Sequence – ANSWERS

1. chimney
2. grouper
3. beret
4. 343
5. sparta
6. fibula
7. I
8. R
9. stapes
10. galaxy

| 4-5 | Average | 8-9 | Very good |
| 6-7 | Good | 10 | Exceptional |

VERBAL TEST 4

PART X

Classification

Classification is where a group of objects or ideas include one word which does not belong to that group. You have to select that word from each of the groups.

Example   pine, fir, elm, spruce, hemlock

Answer: ELM is a hardwood, the remainder are softwoods.

You have six minutes in which to select your ten words.

1. virago, scorpion, wasp, bee, hornet
2. collyrium, mascara, barette, lipsalve, kohl
3. statuette, figurine, mezzotint, statue, bust
4. rontgen, X-ray, gamma, cosmic, lambent
5. gutter, anemometer, gargoyle, scupper, culvert
6. bacteria, microbe, germ, virus, amoeba
7. minion, lackey, flunkey, sirdar, henchman
8. caboose, pinnace, ketch, felucca, caique
9. lurcher, mastodon, mastiff, whippet, beagle
10. staccato, crescendo, diminuendo, impetigo, pianissimo

VERBAL TEST 4

PART X

Classification — ANSWERS

1. virago
2. barette
3. mezzotint
4. lambent
5. anemometer
6. amoeba
7. sirdar
8. caboose
9. mastodon
10. impetigo

4-5	Average		8-9	Very good
6-7	Good		10	Exceptional

TOTAL SCORE VERBAL TEST 4

40-59	Average		80-90	Very good
60-79	Good		91-100	Exceptional